Abide

Resting in the Unfailing Love of God

Cover design by Kristen Ingebretson
Edited by Jennifer Van Metre
Interior design by Tobi Carter

ISBN 978-1-6868-0649-0 (paperback)

www.katiekibbe.com

Abide

Resting in the Unfailing Love of God

Katie Kibbe

Contents

Introduction

At heart we are nurturers, warriors, hard working companions, road builders, and bridge menders. The majority of our days are spent helping others. Educated and highly respected in circles both large and small, we can throw together a meal with a moment's notice, baby on our hip, while fielding phone calls and monitoring homework. We are expert multitaskers and problem solvers taking pride in our productivity.

Raised to believe that we could have it all and do it all, we think we should enjoy every moment of the process. In our effort to live up to our full potential, we burn the candle at both ends rising early to make a hot breakfast, staying up late to make sure that last load of laundry is folded. Yet, we don't understand why we are so tired.

Our weariness affects our internal monologue distracting us with discouragement rather than directing us toward hope. We want to experience joy and love others fully, but some days joy is elusive and love is fleeting as we struggle to manage all that needs to be done with a smile.

Our hearts and souls want to rest and refuel in beauty and truth, yet we are surrounded by discord and conflict. We may even struggle to make meaningful connections in a world of superficial relationships. There are many great seasons of life. Sadly, some days we feel like we are paddling upstream with a toothpick as our family relaxes in the back of the boat, urging us to paddle faster.

Turning to experts for tips on how to work more efficiently or productively, we make more lists and buy better planners. Spiritual writers tell us to pray more often. Despite following the advice, we end up discouraged when we reach the end of another day snapping at those we claim to love the most. It is hard to know what to do, especially with the laundry to be done and bills to be paid.

What if we are looking for answers in all the wrong places? What if the source of joy and peace is not found in increased efficiency and productivity? What if true joy, love, and peace come not from doing more but from taking a step back?

God's immense and merciful love for you is revealed in the person of Jesus. You no longer need to rely upon your achievements and accolades in order to receive and live in His love, peace, and joy. Abiding with Jesus, *resting* in His love, allows your soul to regenerate and refuel so that you can go about the work of revealing the Kingdom of God here on earth.

Like you, I am proficient at juggling a lot of tasks and enjoy staying busy, thriving when I am needed. Unfortunately, this system is only sustainable for so long. Relocating after the children went to college, I was forced to trade in my packed planner, exchanging it instead for a calendar full of empty spaces.

With the gift of time, I began to wonder what it looked like to love my people when I could not show my love through productivity. Instead of consulting the latest life advice from a best-selling guru, I decided to go to the source of love and consult the best book of life wisdom, the Bible.

I started where you would probably start, St. Paul's letter to the Corinthians. You know the passage, *Love is patient, love is kind.* (1 Corinthians 13:4) Paul provides us a laundry list of do's and don'ts related to love, ending with the reminder that love never fails. Wiping the tears from my eyes, I recognized the distance between my heart: a heart performing to earn love and the heart of God: a heart characterized by an outpouring of mercy and compassion.

To understand St. Paul's advice on a more personal level, I needed help, a bridge to get to the other side of the valley. There was clearly work to be done in my heart if I was going to learn to love in a way that did not require me to be in constant motion. Does any of this sound familiar?

Around the same time, a friend mentioned she would like a new Scripture study focused on the women in the bible. This was not the first time she had asked for my take on their experiences. I was hesitant. There are some women and many topics I would rather not dwell on. I put her off, again, telling her that other people are better equipped to tackle that topic. She pushed back and encouraged me to ponder her request instead of reflexively declining.

Eventually, fond memories of my days walking the halls of my all girl high school flooded my mind, and I started to think that spending time with these women might not be so bad after all.

What I thought was going to teach me how to be a "better person" ended up giving me a more intimate view into the loving and merciful heart of Jesus. As I explored each woman's story, I marveled at how open and aware Jesus was about her unique circumstances. How could a man be like this? I was amazed at how each woman responded to Him, as well. How was she not afraid to talk to Him? In each instance, there was no fear, no hesitancy. Their behavior did not align with how I anticipated I would act if I were to meet Jesus in person.

Day after day spent poring over the stories of Jesus and these women, I noticed how He spoke to them and how they reached out to Him. I also recognized the times where my faith and understanding of Jesus' character did not align with my own internal monologue. And so, *Abide* was born.

We have spent far too many days being independent and emotionally unavailable to the One who can heal and transform our souls. It is time to reacquaint ourselves with Jesus' love and accept His invitation to Abide with Him. Jesus is the bridge between a life of self-focused dissatisfaction to a life of self-donative love.

As you work through the lessons in *Abide*, you will begin to recognize some of the obstacles which have prevented you from fully accepting and resting in God's love in the past. Familiar with your particular speed bump, you will be equipped to spot it from further away and avoid it in the future. You will grow and trust that remaining with Jesus is a better solution than managing life on your own. You will discover new ways to fuel your soul so that you are better prepared to handle life's difficulties with love and grace rather than bitterness and disillusionment. Life's obstacles are much easier to overcome when you approach them, with Jesus, from a place of rest rather than exhaustion.

Many women think an intimate relationship with Jesus is reserved for the spiritual elite, someone with a certain theological pedigree, or a lot of time on her hands. You might believe that a deeper relationship requires unpleasant effort, striving, or knowledge of novenas. This could not be further from the truth. You already have what you need, right now, to experience the love, joy, and peace God wants to share with you.

God did not create you to live a spiritually mediocre life. He created you to be a vessel for His love, a conduit of His mercy, and a light for the world. Now is the time to take a step back, rest, and rediscover His unfailing love for you so that you can reveal Him to those around you.

Jesus sees you. He knows how you are tempted to hide from Him behind a mask of perfection or busyness. He loves you. He patiently waits to reveal His love and wants to draw you into a deeper, more meaningful relationship with Himself. Jesus longs to fill you with His love and His peace. He wants for you to experience His joy, regardless of the difficult circumstances you might be facing. His love is powerful, uncontainable, and unfailing.

The women in Abide were singularly focused on Jesus and did not allow their burdens, fears, or worries to stop them from approaching Him. They remained with Him accepting His love and walked away utterly transformed.

Now is the time for you to take a small step back, rest, and abide with Jesus and His unfailing love.

Abide: A guidebook for your Spiritual journey.

Where are you dwelling? Do you fall prey to doubt, distraction, and discouragement rather than dwelling in the peace and unfailing love of Jesus? Do you linger in the past with regret and disappointment instead of living with confidence and courage? Or, are you generally satisfied with how things are going, yet feel as though there should be something more?

Wherever you are, today is the perfect time to Abide.

Jesus' love encourages, endures, uplifts, and strengthens. He invites you to patiently persevere in your current circumstances with joy rather than gritting your teeth and white knuckling it until the end of the day.

As you learn to Abide with Jesus, you will discover how to:

1. Wait for Him;
2. Submit to Him;
3. Dwell with Him; and
4. Remain faithful to Him.

This guidebook gives you the tools you need to abide with Jesus. You will meet Him in a new way through the eyes of your sisters in faith both from Scripture and recent history. By prayerfully pondering the words of Scripture and reflecting on your life, the Holy Spirit will enable you to release your burdens and recognize God's unfailing love for you.

I hope you fall in love with Jesus either for the first time or once again. I want you to see that God's love for you is never ending and never failing. Rest in His love and allow Him to transform your life.

Nuts and Bolts of Abide

Each chapter of Abide is broken down into segments. You can work through the chapter all at once, or do a little bit at a time throughout the week as your schedule allows. Consider gathering with a group of friends to journey through this book together. I am often amazed at how the Holy Spirit uses other people in conversation to guide me to the next step in my own faith journey.

Introduction
A real life reflection highlighting common obstacles you might encounter when abiding with Jesus.

Women of Faith/Devotions/Gratitude
The second section rotates giving you an opportunity to discover a new prayer practice, a sister in faith, or something new for which to be grateful.

Scripture
The Holy Spirit speaks to us through the Word. Prayerfully approach these passages, reading them with fresh eyes and an open heart. Consider reading them through twice before answering the questions. Look for details you may have missed as you heard the passage read to you in the past.

Putting It into Practice
Here you will find ideas on incorporating prayer into your busy day. Whether you have an extra 5, 10, or 15 minutes a life of abiding with Jesus is grounded in conversation with Him.

Prayer Intentions
If you are using *Abide* in a group, use this page to record a prayer intention for each member, every week. If you are working through the book on your own, use this page to record your personal prayer intentions for the week. When you pick up *Abide*, you can return to these pages to remember your connection to the body of Christ.

One

Unfailing Love

You shall seek the Lord your God, and you shall find Him when you search after Him with your whole heart and your whole soul. Deuteronomy 4:29

Introduction

Like all children, I loved to imagine what Christmas morning would look like at my house. In my mind, I could picture myself walking into the living room and there, amid the brightly wrapped gifts each with a beautiful hand tied bow, would be my "Big Present". The room would be dark except for the glow from the lights on the tree and the spotlight pointing to the big box. These fantasies were sparked, I'm sure, by ads shown in between episodes of Love Boat and Fantasy Island.

The centerpiece present starring in the movie in my mind would change each year. Every Christmas morning, I would wake up earlier and earlier to see if Santa's gifts would live up to my TV commercial induced fantasy. Every year, I suffered a smidge of disappointment. There was no spotlight. The wrapping paper was not glamorous. Disenchanted following a thorough inspection of the gifts Santa so neatly laid out on the sofa, the only thing left to do in the pitch black before dawn was watch Davey and Goliath reruns on TV as I waited for the rest of my family to wake up.

Did you have television advertising fueled expectations of Santa, as well? Visions that were impossible to recreate without a staff and budget that exceeds the GDP of a small country.

Once I discovered the true source of the Christmas presents, I realized why the presents Santa left for the TV children were wrapped and presented so much more extravagantly than the gifts under my tree. We did not do extravagant in my family. My mother worked hard to surprise us and we never lacked for anything, yet my imagination always had the ability to outrun the excitement of my reality. So, in order to avoid the deflation, which accompanied my disappointment, I lowered my expectations. As I abandoned the hope of discovering joy on Christmas morning, I began to sleep later and later each Christmas morning. Like so many other teenagers, I was jaded.

So, I turned my imagination elsewhere. Instead of hoping for a big joy filled present from Santa, I began to look for the excitement of the grand gesture in another area of my life. The influential images transitioned from Christmas commercials to TV shows or movies. Without quite realizing it, I imagined the scenes I saw depicted on the screen, which brought the heroine to tears would satisfy some deep longing in my own heart. Did you ever go to a movie and come home with a new idea of what true love looks like?

I waited for the guy outside my window holding the boom box to declare his love for me. I imagined Jake from Sixteen Candles, driving up in his Porsche to reveal his secret crush on me. Or, the handsome, misunderstood dance instructor falling in love with me as we dazzled everyone with our synchronicity on the dance floor. Maybe, I could travel across the ocean on a steamer named the Titanic and meet my one true love, the one who would look in my eyes and just get me. The one who would risk his own safety to ensure my own.

With each movie, my mind would create these outlandish images of what it looks like to reveal your love to someone. Whether it was the grand gesture or outrageous gift, big was on the agenda.

When fantasies eclipse reality, we are left disappointed and disillusioned as people fail to live up to our unreasonable expectations. Instead of drawing me into a deeper understanding of the world, my imagination eventually created barriers, which made recognizing love difficult.

You see, no-one could match the image of love that I created in my mind. Now, intellectually I knew that these images of love were strictly happening in movies and were not based in reality. Yet, my heart imagined that someday, somehow someone would go out of their way to reveal their love for me with some enormous grand gesture.

As my life failed to unfold in the exact way I imagined, I was disappointed. I began to believe that there was something wrong with me, that I was not worthy of love from anyone outside of my family. I looked at life around me in my high school and early college days where I had a front row seat to view many broken relationships and shattered friendships. I thought to myself: Love Fails.

We have each experienced, in countless ways, that truth that love is hard. People are limited and self-centered by nature. They disappoint and hurt us. If we are honest, we recognize the countless ways that we too, have failed and hurt others. Statistics show the rates of divorce, the number of parents who abandon children, and the unconscionable amount of genocide in this world. Our hearts have been broken and we ache at times from our contact with other people. Some mornings it is enticing to imagine wrapping ourselves in bubble wrap before we even get out of bed to protect our hearts from the onslaught of the day.

Thinking love originates from and is controllable by humans, it is easy to lose hope in love due to our extensive experience of past love fails. We retreat behind walls created to shelter our fragile hearts. We isolate ourselves behind superficial niceness accepting mediocrity in exchange for playing it safe. We separate others into groups picking and choosing who will be the beneficiary of our attention.

Because we are saturated with imagery from a media driven culture with a high emphasis on the virtual, it is easy for us to be confused about what love looks like in real life. We may not even realize how we are influenced by what we read and watch. Without a proper counterbalance, we maintain unrealistic expectations of ourselves and others in the area of interpersonal relationships.

Our image of God is based upon what we experience in the everyday.

We assign the same human qualities that we experience in our daily lives to God because of our limited imaginations. Unrealized dreams and our own past experiences with heartbreak make it extremely difficult to understand the nature of God's unfailing love. Consequently, most of us struggle to accept that He loves us each individually. So, we hold unspoken prayers in a locked box in our heart, afraid that giving words to our deepest desire will only lead to more disappointment.

Love happens when and where we least expect to find it. While we might be looking for the grand gesture, unfailing love is most often revealed in the sacrificial actions we fail to notice because they are offered in such quiet, subtle ways.

Glimpses of sacrificial love give us hope that there is something more available than the mediocre life for which we might be tempted to settle. But, we must be living in such a way that our eyes have the opportunity to recognize what occurs out of the spotlight and in packages, which are not so neatly wrapped. Waiting, an integral part of abiding, is often necessary in order to experience authentic love. Sadly, we are no longer skilled in this most necessary art.

In order to recognize unfailing love and desire to abide with Jesus there, we need to live slowly so that we can be on the lookout for love rather than channeling all of our energy into protecting our hearts from potential offenses and heartache. We need to foster our own patience so that we will long to submit to, dwell with, and remain faithful to the One Who endures. Abandoning fantasies and pessimism sparked by heartache opens your eyes to the reality which is right in front of you: God's Unfailing Love is available for you right now.

The pages of Scripture reveal that God's love never fails. He is the author of the grand gesture and the ultimate sacrifice. Your imagination is intrigued by the sweeping romantic gesture because God created you to respond to the most love saturated grand gesture of all time: Jesus' sacrifice on the cross. Remaining with Jesus, abiding in His love rather than the cheap substitute offered in most movies and reality programs will lead you to the experience of joy, which surpasses all understanding. God's Unfailing Love is revealed in the life of Jesus. When we allow His sacrifice to capture our hearts and the entirety of our imagination, our lives are transformed.

Unfailing Love grows from a seed planted in your soul by the Holy Spirit and nurtured by conversations with Jesus in prayer. It spills out of you in ways you never before thought possible. His love opens your eyes to view the world from an entirely new vantage point of hope. His love heals, redeems, and transforms. His love forgives sins and welcomes you home. His love fills you with the confidence to rest with Him and empowers you to rise up and make His love known in new ways that are uniquely your own.

We know love when we see it, yet nurturing dormant seeds of love is hard without a play book. The best play book I know is the Bible. Yet, we have mastered the art of making excuses about why we can't spend time abiding with Jesus. It is time to lay our excuses aside and allow the Holy Spirit to reveal Jesus to you in the Word. Are you ready to Abide with Jesus?

Questions

1. Have you ever imagined that God is similar to Santa, watching out and only giving gifts to the good little girls?

2. Are there times in the past when you were disappointed on Christmas morning? Did you blame Santa or did you blame yourself for not being "good enough" when Santa was watching?

3. Are there seasons in your life that unfolded in a way you did not like? Who did you blame?

4. Why do you think our imaginations are captured by the romantic grand gestures we see on TV, in movies, or books? Is this something God placed within us so that we might pursue Him?

5. How does heartbreak or disappointment affect our understanding of the love of God?

6. Who is the true source of love?

7. What happens when we think that the only source of love is other people?

8. What are some things we chase after that are cheap substitutes for the love of God and ultimately fail to satisfy our innate desire for love?

9. Do you need more rest? What is one thing you can set aside to spend more time in silence?

10. What obstacles do you think are standing in the way of your entering into a deeper relationship with Jesus and abiding in His love?

Gratitude

Shout praises to the LORD! He is good to us, and his love never fails.
Psalm 107:1 (Contemporary English Version)

When we are looking at life from a glass half empty perspective, it is easy to become discouraged. Gratitude, giving thanks to God, retrains our brain to look for all of the ways that God is actively pursuing our love. He often pursues us though other people. What are three small things another person has done for you, which has revealed love? Don't feel like you need to stop at three if you can think of more.

1.

2.

3.

Scripture

*But God proves His love for us in that while we were still
sinners, Christ died for us. Romans 5:8*

In Jesus' time, women were not considered trustworthy enough to relate eye-witness testimony under oath. Not only were they cast to the margins of society with limited property rights, access to education, and nominal ability to earn a living, women did not enjoy the same freedoms as men. Jesus defies cultural norms and elevates women by entering into relationships with them.

In three of the Gospels, Mary Magdalene is the first person to talk to Jesus after His resurrection. Discrepancies exist in the details of Jesus' crucifixion, burial and resurrection. The details make it difficult to arrive at one solid historical narrative description of what happened to whom and when on the morning that the tomb was found empty.

When we are looking for the Unfailing Love of God in Scripture, we do not read the bible for historical accuracy. Instead, we look at the big picture. Often the details, which remain consistent across all four Gospel accounts, can heighten our awareness that something is important. In each Gospel, Magdalene, drawn by love, went to the tomb, found it empty, and was the first person to talk to Jesus. She is then propelled to share the good news with the apostles.

The name Magdalene is thought by some to be a reference to her hometown. Other scholars believe that Magdalene was a nickname associated with her profession or personality. Unfortunately, Magdalene was cast as a prostitute in one sermon by Pope Gregory, which negatively influenced many peoples' opinions of her over time.

Despite this reputation, St. Thomas Aquinas called Magdalene, the Apostle to the Apostles, as she delivered the Resurrection message to the apostles. The Dominican order of priests and sisters look at Magdalene as a co-patroness because of her presence at the resurrection and her willingness to share the good news so quickly with others.

She is the patron saint of converts, hairstylists, perfumers, penitents, and women. Her feast day, July 22, is on par with that of the feasts of the other apostles.

*But Mary Magdalene and the other Mary remained sitting
there, facing the tomb. Matthew 27:61*

Read Luke 8:1-8

1. Who accompanied Jesus?

2. What does Luke say ailed Mary Magdalene? Is there any indication from this passage that Mary struggled with sexual sins?

3. Have you ever thought about the role women played in Jesus' ministry? Does this passage surprise you?

4. Does the way that the sower spreads the seed change the nature of the seed? Is it the same regardless of where it lands?

5. What does the seed need in order to become what it is truly meant to be?

Read Matthew 28:1-10

6. Who came to see the tomb?

7. Why and how did they leave?

8. What happened on their way to talk to the disciples?

9. What did the women do?

10. When have you seen women at Jesus' feet in Scripture?

11. How long did Mary Magdalene wait between the burial and going to attend to Jesus' body?

Putting It Into Practice

Today is the day you are going to kick all excuses to the curb and commit to yourself and Jesus that you will Abide with Him.

Slowing down is the first step.

You do not need to slam on the brakes though. Slowing down means easing your foot off the accelerator. Do this by removing one activity from your to do list; reallocate your time so that you are able to enjoy spending more time with Jesus. This is easier when there are fewer objects floating in your peripheral vision to distract you.

As you abide or wait with Jesus steep your soul in the words of Scripture. His living water will well up from within, hydrating and invigorating you as you linger in the silence. Relish your time with Him each day and allow Him to rewrite the stories that capture your imagination and allow Him to heal your heart.

Listen to what the Holy Spirit says to you in Scripture, what touches you, what moves you to action? Can you agree with what Jesus is saying to you? Invite Him into your day and allow Him to dwell with you as you move about fulfilling your responsibilities. Relax in His presence and know that you are deeply loved and cherished.

If you have 5 minutes, Pray:

Oh Jesus.   I love You.
Thank You for calling me here today.
I am grateful for the many ways You have
revealed Yourself to me throughout my life.
I invite You to sit with me and teach me to rest.
I humbly ask You to show me Your immense love
in a way that my little heart can understand.
Strengthen my resolve to set aside the time
to encounter you in Scripture
so that I may understand
Your Unfailing Love
for me.
Amen.

If you have 10 minutes, Ponder:

What feels like the death of a dream is possibly the birth of something that will make your soul sing even more beautifully. I think about Mary Magdalene weighed down with oil and spices as she went to do her work at the tomb of our Savior. She was grieving, yet doing what she knew to do next.

Amazed that the stone is moved, she runs away to tell the news to the other disciples. While on her way, she sees Jesus and falls to His feet to adore Him. She must have laid her burden down at the tomb. Mary could neither run with her hands full, nor could she reach out and touch Jesus if she was still holding on to her vision of what was "supposed" to happen. Mary was nimble enough to pivot. What are the oils and spices that Jesus needs you to set down so that you can reach out and touch Him in a new way?

If you have 15 minutes, Act:

Almighty God, whose blessed Son restored Mary Magdalene to health of body and of mind, and called her to be a witness of His resurrection: Mercifully grant that by your grace we may be healed from all our infirmities and know You in the power of His unending life; who with you and the Holy Spirit lives and reigns, one God, now and for ever. Amen. *Collect from Feast of St. Mary Magdalene. Anglican Church.*

Journal your thoughts about this prayer.

Prayer Intentions

Two

What's Holding You Back?

*Remain in My love...I have told you this so that My joy may be
in you and your joy may be complete. John 15:9b,11*

Introduction

You want more intimate relationships, whether it is with Jesus or the many people you love. Yet the pathway is rocky and strewn with obstacles. You may lack confidence in yourself and might be unsure whether you have the courage to change in order to live the life of love that Jesus exemplifies.

In a world where we play it safe in prayer, it is hard to imagine that a deeper, richer experience of love is available this side of heaven. Instead of embracing the Unfailing Love that Jesus offers, we accept spiritually mediocre lives, busying ourselves with much that does not have eternal value. God wants us to experience His Unfailing Love, yet we hold onto our mistaken concepts of love, afraid of change.

Many of us have not yet taken Jesus as seriously as our souls would like. We carry burdens that are heavy and difficult to manage. These burdens preoccupy our hearts and minds making it difficult to rest and inhibiting our ability to love wholeheartedly.

Fear drives much of our relationship with Jesus. Most of us are comfortable keeping Jesus at arm's length. We are afraid of what He will see if we allow ourselves to be known. Others of us are afraid of what we might be asked to do once we go all in with Jesus.

So we keep our distance. We struggle to abide and rest with Jesus.

Instead of waiting, we run ahead of Him chasing our calling. Instead of submitting to His love, we control. Instead of dwelling with Him, remaining in contact with Jesus throughout the day, we distract ourselves with busyness. We are faithful, but only some of the time.

Many of us relate to Jesus in much the same way as we treated our best friend's brother when we were growing up. You know, the one you saw occasionally, knew about from other people, and spoke to intermittently. You related to him through another person, either your friend or your sibling. Maybe he intimidated you because he could drive when you were still riding a bike. Or, he embarrassed you when he was around because he was a little quirky and all the cool girls rolled their eyes at him. You might have gotten close enough to follow on social media, yet you never gave him your phone number.

Love Requires Time And Vulnerability.

We might mistakenly believe we can only know about Jesus from the spare descriptions of his interaction with other people in the Bible. Looking at His life as a series of episodes read for us each Sunday, we are tempted to imagine Jesus as just a great guy, a healer, a miracle worker, a charismatic teacher, a revolutionary, maybe a man for others, just not for me personally. Not realizing we are mistaken about Whom He is and how we truly come to know His heart, we often take His lessons, yet leave His love behind.

Our confusion and disillusion become barriers in recognizing His unfailing love. Our relationship with Him remains superficial as we speed read the black letters on a page of Scripture, close our bible, and move to the next thing on our list.

Transitioning from acquaintance to friendship and eventually into an intimate love relationship with Jesus takes time, honesty, and effort. It requires that we come to know His character and what true Unfailing Love means. In order to want to give our lives to Him, we have to know Who it is that we intend to walk alongside day in and day out.

Jesus reveals Himself to individuals in conversation throughout the Gospels. He performs miracles and brings hope to many who are weary from carrying the burdens of life. Jesus gives Himself to us today in the Eucharist.

He talks to us in Adoration and in prayer. He goes to the margins and seeks out the ones outside of the spotlight's reach.

With each successive day, as you show up to talk to Jesus, the Holy Spirit deepens your relationship. As you allow Him to sit with you, trust grows. He works as the gardener of your heart and your soul, tending to the seeds of holiness planted there long ago.

In order to immerse ourselves in the Unfailing Love of God, we must come to know Jesus more intimately. Now is the time to engage in your love story in a new way in order to rise above the mediocrity.

To understand the unfailing love of God, we must:

· Imagine what happens in the white space between the black letters of Scripture;
· Enjoy time walking with Jesus, seeing how He interacts with other women;
· Listen to Him speak;
· Rest as He draws you in;
· Remove the bubble wrap from around your heart and allow yourself to fall in love with Him;
· Allow Him to touch the tender spots where you are bruised;
· Invite Him to heal your wounds;
· Recognize the dirt caked on His feet; and
· Be so moved by His presence that you can't stop yourself from wanting to tend to Him.

As you come to a deeper understanding and acceptance of the Unfailing Love of Jesus, you will discover that He will never disappoint you.

It has taken years to improve the quality of images in movies and television. What used to be grainy black and white pictures are now so clear that you can see the pores on an actor's face. Transitioning from seeing Jesus as a character in a black and white program to one you view in High Definition takes time. But it is so very worth every ounce of energy you devote to this journey.

It takes time to fall in love with someone so deeply that you would want to wash the donkey droppings off His feet with your tears as women did for Jesus. Opening your heart enough that you would walk away from your life as you know it to follow Him does not happen in an instant. The women in Jesus' life sat at His feet and listened to Him talk. It is vital that we sit at Jesus' feet as well. Resting with Him will help you discover how to release what you used to think was important so that you can now learn what He thinks is necessary.

Time, The One Asset We Think Is In Shortest Supply.

Growing into a deeper relationship with Jesus takes time and we think we have none left to give. Depending upon where you are in life, the obligations you have with work and family, you may have more or less to offer than others. The amazing thing about God is that he accepts what we have to offer so long as we offer it to Him. Instead of resting on your excuses, accept the challenge to lay down your burdens and allow Him to love you.

Dedicate a few minutes each day to Him in silence and stillness. Wait on Him. Slow down, read the Gospels and see how Jesus treats each woman He meets. Answer the questions in your study so that your imagination is engaged in His story. Invite Him into your day as you discover new things for which to be grateful. Be inspired to rise up and walk alongside Him. Learn how each woman loved Him uniquely. See all of the ways that He loved them, too. Imagine what happens in the gaps in the stories, in the details that are left off the page.

Jesus' Unfailing Love exceeds all that we can imagine. As you become more familiar with the nuances of Jesus' personality, you will recognize that His love is more than merely patient and kind. He is more than forgiveness. Jesus' love seeks to heal, lift up, and restore. His love looks to the individual person and the greater society in which that individual lives. He knows that something greater lies ahead and that doubt and discouragement are mere distractions from the greater journey.

Jesus' love is Unfailing and He is waiting for you to discover just how magnificent He really is. Abandon spiritual mediocrity and come to know Jesus as Mary Magdalene did so that your heart is drawn to the tomb before the sun rises because you can't imagine there is anywhere else that you would rather be.

God's love for you could not be contained by death. His love is so powerful that it rolled back the stone which covered the tomb, and Jesus walked out. So much of what Jesus did went unwitnessed and unnoticed. His Incarnation in the still silence, along with His Resurrection in the dark were intended to capture your heart and your imagination. Allow these mysterious grand gestures to spark your imagination. Abide with Him and discover the joy that accompanies His Unfailing Love.

Questions

1. Have you ever imagined coming to know Jesus on a deeper level? Do you think this is possible?

2. What are 3 things that you could begin to do that will help you come to know Jesus on a deeper level? Circle one that you are able to do this week.

3. Are you waiting for Jesus to extend a grand gesture, a big reveal, some sort of lightening bolt experience before you make the necessary changes to your schedule in order to spend more time with Him?

4. What are some of the ways people become disillusioned by love?

5. Do you see a connection between your view of the frailty of human love and your possible hesitancy to accept the fullness of God's love?

6. How would you describe your relationship with Jesus?
   A. Acquaintances
   B. Friends
   C. Dating
   D. In love
   E. It's complicated

7. We see Mary Magdalene arrive at the tomb with a few things. If you were to go to the tomb to tend to Jesus' body, how do you think you would arrive at the tomb: empty handed, both hands full, pulling a suitcase full of supplies, or driving up with a loaded down SUV?

8. What we carry to the tomb can be a metaphor for how we approach growing deeper in our relationship with Jesus. Spiritual writers often focus on the impact that material goods have on our relationship with Jesus. While this is true, we fail to recognize how our emotional baggage stands in our way, preventing us from embracing the feet of Christ and adoring Him. What are some of the emotional wounds which might inhibit someone from reaching out to Jesus and accepting His love?

9. Does the term spiritual mediocrity resonate with you? What does this term mean to you?

10. We have read or heard stories of God giving a "word" to someone, or know of apparitions. What happens when we don't hear God speak to us, or have a deep mystical experience? Do we think that an intimate relationship with God is not available to us? Maybe we think we are lacking something essential, that we are not "enough" for God?

11. Mary Magdalene approached the tomb with her oils and spices prepared for the tasks of the day that she imagined awaited her behind the stone. When she arrived, she discovered a new reality. She dropped what she brought leaving her hands empty to embrace the new reality Jesus reveals. What are the oils and spices you need to lay down so that you can pursue Jesus?

12. It is hard to understand what it must have been like to connect
     with Jesus in real life. He lived in such a different time and culture
     than we do. It is so easy to dismiss Him as irrelevant when our lives
     move at such a different pace. So, we are tempted to leave Him on the
     page and not engage with Him in our real life. What are some of the
     excuses you have given in the past about why you are unable to pray
     daily, finish your Scripture Study lessons, or ponder Scripture?

Women of Faith

They who wait for the Lord shall renew their strength, they shall mount up with wings like eagles, they shall run and not be weary, they shall walk and not faint. Isaiah 40:31 (RSVCE)

Role models and mentors are extremely valuable when we are charting a new course, especially when it is unfamiliar. The Women of Faith you will meet were able to Abide with Jesus despite the obstacles life threw in their path. They show us what it looks like to continue to love in the seasons when answers are not readily available and the path is not as clear-cut and straightforward as we would like. There are so many women who have given their lives to God through their loving service to the poor, the sick, and the marginalized. They figured out how to combine resting in God's love along with active service to others in order to not just survive but to thrive. They learned that it was possible to find a rhythm of life that worked so that they could use all that He had given them to help others.

One year after the publication of Nathaniel Hawthorne's classic novel *The Scarlet Letter*, his wife Sophia gave birth to a little girl named Rose. Raised among the literary greats of the late 1800's, the family travelled throughout Europe where Rose received a good education. Following the death of both of her parents, she married George Lathrop in an Anglican Church. Sadly, their only child died from diphtheria when he was 5 years old.

Rose and George converted to Catholicism when they returned to the States, which was quite the scandal among their friends. Over time, George began to abuse not only alcohol, but Rose herself. Afraid for her safety, Rose obtained permission from the church to separate from George. He died a few years later from complications of his alcohol abuse.

Instead of allowing heartache and heartbreak to isolate her into a world of comfort, Rose remained open to ways that God was inviting her to grow in His love for her and reveal that same love to other people. Rose discovered that when poor people, especially women, were diagnosed with cancer, they were often sent to a home, separated from their families, receiving no medical care. Rose was heartbroken when this happened to someone she knew.

The common assumption at the time was that cancer was contagious and few would risk their own health to take care of someone without being paid. Rose was not content to allow these women to be ostracized.

When she was forty-five Rose, trained as a nurse and moved to a very poor area in New York City in order to serve those without access to medical care. Others joined her work, which was funded by donations. Eventually, she bought a home and dedicated her life to the care of poor women with cancer.

A Dominican priest noticed her work and offered her spiritual direction. Eventually, she took vows as a Third Order Dominican. Eventually, other women joined her and looked for a structure to guide their work and prayer.

In 1900, the order of the Dominican Sisters of Hawthorne was approved by the church, and Rose Lathrop took the habit and the name Mother Mary Alphonsa. She died in 1926.

The Sisters continue to run care homes to this day, including the Our Lady of Perpetual Help Home in Atlanta. Mother Alphonsa has been recognized as a Servant of God and her cause of canonization is underway.

Mother Alphonsa could easily have given in to the disillusionment and discouragement that comes with grief as a result of the loss of her parents, young child, and the abuse of her husband. Despite her pain, she moved forward keeping her eyes on the road ahead. Her relationship with God fueled her ability to continue loving, which gave birth to a beautiful ministry of compassionate caregiving for the terminally ill.

Scripture

Be still before the Lord; wait for Him. Psalm 37:7

Another word for abide is to remain or wait. Just as Magdalene remains with Jesus at the tomb, so we must remain or abide with Jesus in our every day lives. This requires us to be nimble and light on our feet. We must not be encumbered by expectations or fear. When we are tethered to Jesus, He will nourish us and allow our souls to flourish. All we need to do is give Him the space in our calendar and access to our hearts in order for Him to do His healing work.

Read John 20:1-18

1. After the disciples leave the empty tomb, who remains behind? What is she doing?

2. Magdalene sees and speaks with angels, why do you think she was not afraid of them?

3. Who does Magdalene mistake Jesus for in verse 15?

4. Later, Jesus will reveal Himself to the male disciples by showing His wounds (John 20:20), how does Jesus reveal Himself to Magdalene?

5. What does Jesus tell her in verse 16?

6. Why do you think He says these things?

7. Women in Jesus' time were invisible. This became Mary Magdalene's biggest strength in that she could move about unnoticed by those in power. What was Mary Magdalene able to do that the men were afraid to do?

8. We often think that love needs to be showy and on display. Love that happens in the unnoticed corners of life is often more powerful than glittering displays of personality. How does Mary Magdalene reveal her love for Jesus?

Read John 15:1-5

9. With Whom are we to remain?

10. If we remain with Jesus, what does He promise?

11. What is the fruit Jesus describes in verse 5? Give an example.

12. Practically speaking, what does it look like to remain with Jesus? Be as specific as possible.

Putting it into Practice

If you have 5 minutes, Pray:

Oh Jesus, I love You.
Thank You for calling me here today.
I am grateful for the many ways You have
revealed Yourself to me throughout my life.
I welcome You in as the Gardener of my heart and soul.
Tend the seed of faith and love that was planted at my Baptism.
Give me the desire to abide with You as You work.
I humbly ask that You show me Your immense love
in a way that my little heart can understand.
Strengthen my resolve to set aside the time
to encounter You in Scripture so that
I may understand Your Unfailing Love for me.
Amen.

If you have 10 minutes, Ponder:

Jesus, as the gardener of your heart, is able to transform you into someone who loves others with an Unfailing Love. Linger with Him in prayer as He tends the small supernatural seed of grace that was planted at your Baptism. Remain with Him as He waters it with the blood and water that pour from His side. As the seedling sprouts, encounter the Holy Spirit as He blows and strengthens your spiritual roots.

Prayer provides the necessary air and the Sacraments provide the sun allowing this love to expand your soul beyond what you originally thought possible.

He tills the soil and, if you allow Him, pulls the weeds which threaten to choke your growth. At times, you will need to endure as He prunes you, as removing a branch or two will ultimately strengthen your soul. The weeding and pruning are painful, yet necessary. How we respond to the disappointments of each day makes the ultimate difference in whether we grow to experience and exhibit unfailing love or walk away from love.

What part of the gardening process captures your imagination? Ponder this today.

If you have 15 minutes, Act:

Journal your thoughts about this question: What is really holding you back from Jesus?

Prayer Intentions

Three

Patience is a Superpower

Love is patient. 1 Corinthians 13:4

Introduction

With the click of a few buttons, the stroke of a few keys, you can have your groceries delivered to your door without ever changing out of your pajamas. Watching almost any movie or TV show you want is now possible anywhere you find a wifi connection. Need a new book while you are relaxing on the beach? You don't even have to leave the balmy breeze or comfy chair.

Instant everything has changed the way that we view the world. A phone in your pocket means you are accessible 24/7. Texting accelerated the pace of communication virtually eliminating the need for voicemail. Always available, we expect everyone else to respond to our calls, texts, and emails with identical speed.

We no longer have to dedicate time to exercising because leggings now give your thighs the appearance of hours spent at the gym without unnecessary sweat and sore muscles. Serums give your eyes an instant lift. A driver can appear at your door in minutes with dinner from a variety of restaurants.

Instant and immediate are the anthems of our lives. Instant results. Immediate gratification. Unfortunately, instant is an obstacle in the pathway to discover the Unfailing Love of God.

The pace of life and our meals along with changes in fashion and communication have altered the way we think. This shift was gradual enough that you may not even be aware of the impact all of these changes have on your daily outlook. Where waiting had been the norm for most of our lives, we are now indignant if we are asked to wait for anything.

I did not recognize my own addiction to the instant until I moved. The pace of life in South Carolina is recognizably slower than life in Atlanta. At first, the differences were glaring. People would not return calls or emails immediately, the pace of a conversation was like a slow stroll through countryside, and Mass was an extra 20-25 minutes longer each week. No-one is ever in a rush to do anything in South Carolina. Adapting to the slow pace of life meant developing a new level of patience.

Where I had grown accustomed to same day delivery, I now have to wait if I order something online - sometimes more than a week. This sounds trivial as I sit here writing these words but, if you live in an area where Amazon has same day delivery, you get used to having what you want, when you want it, as soon as you think you want it. Spoiled, I know. At first I thought it was extravagant to order something in the morning and have it delivered by the afternoon. But, then I got used to the convenience of not having to shop in several places hoping to find the one elusive item. In detoxing from my addiction to instant, I discovered that there is a lot I was missing when I no longer had to wait.

The measure of our daily life can be so rapid that we may not realize that our patience muscle has grown weak and is well on its way to atrophying. How are you doing in the patience department? Do you find this muscle so very easy to flex that everyone in your family comments, "She has the patience of a saint?" Or, are you more like me, stirring in my pew as the one hour mark comes and goes while we sing yet another verse of yet another song?

If you too are struggling with your addiction to instant everything, it is time to grow in patience with yourself, God, and others. If we want to abide with Jesus, we need to learn how to wait.

We all struggle with exhibiting the patience needed to navigate life. There are days when the person we are least patient with is ourself. We demand much of ourselves in so many areas and are frustrated when we are not successful in living up to our own high expectations. We speak to ourselves with more words of shame and condemnation rather than love and affirmation. Some might find it easier to berate themselves instead of building themselves up. In the silence, we may ask: Why am I not more disciplined, successful, holier, stronger, nicer, thinner? Why can't I be a better wife, mother, daughter, sister, or friend? The bitter root of this negativity is impatience.

Those who are closest to us often experience our impatience first hand. Our families are the recipients of our sharp tone, our stony silence, our cutting remarks, or shaking finger. We love these people, unfortunately, when we are disappointed in ourselves, our nerves are raw and we lash out. After we walk away from an encounter that has pushed our buttons, so to speak, we often feel ashamed of our behavior and beat ourselves up for our lack of patience. This starts the cycle all over again.

We are also impatient with God. We have heard it said a million times: God's timing is not our timing. What we want to happen immediately, sometimes He intends for later. God works in our lives each and every day. Unfortunately, if our hearts are not attuned to His, we find it difficult to wait on Him. When we lack patience trusting that God is working all things for our good (Romans 8:28), we take matters in our own hands rather than trusting God to provide for us. We look elsewhere for answers rather than resting in prayer and silence. When we are impatient with God, we fall into our bad coping habits, which often damage our relationship with ourselves and others.

Waiting feels like a waste of time. But, it is precisely in the waiting we discover God is hard at work.

Impatience is an impediment to accepting the love of God, which heals. Patience is a superpower that attracts God's love to you like a magnet and allows it to flow out to others. Living in patience, seeing yourself (and others) through eyes of mercy and love rather than judgment and condemnation, gives your soul room to breathe and space to truly flourish. God's love can fill you with the grace you need to be patient with yourself and others.

So much in life takes longer to unfold than we would like. We need to move through life at a slower pace and anticipate that things will take longer than we might originally think. It takes more time than we often allow to learn a new skill or forgive another person. When we mentally budget more time than we originally anticipate, we are less apt to be disappointed in ourselves and others, which curtails our negative self talk. This, in turn, allows us to remain open to God and others able to accept and reveal His love.

When our expectations are aligned with God's reality, it is easier for us to maintain our inner peace and not become agitated. We are liberated to recognize and share God's love generously with others. When we patiently abide with Jesus, we experience the joy of waiting on Him for direction rather than charging ahead with our own plans.

Jesus was never in a rush and we can learn to wait by pondering His movements. Daily prayer is an exercise in patience, which makes it easier to recognize God in the small moments of your day and accept His love. God reveals Himself to us slowly and patience is essential in order to observe and ponder the clues He reveals.

Looking past the immediate gratification we have come to expect, we see the beauty of gradual growth and change. In the slow, you have time to notice more details in your day. You are able to listen to another with both your ears and your heart. You see the person on the sidelines when, before, your eyes were trained straight ahead, your body propelled toward the next goal.

As we gain a greater appreciation for the value of putting in the patient daily hard work toward a goal, we recognize that tiny steps put together make for a great journey.

Questions

1. What are some of the things in your life that you waited for in the past, which are now delivered instantly?

2. How has "instant everything" affected your ability to accept slow soul growth?

3. Who are you least patient with: God, yourself, or others?

4. Think about a typical day, what causes you to lose your peace? When are you most impatient?

5. What area of your life would you like an extra dose of patience?

6. Looking back over the past several years, what are some small changes you made which have produced positive outcomes?

7. How is daily prayer an exercise in patience?

8. Is patience foundational to love? How so?

9. Some of us are naturally more patient than others. Do you have any tips, tricks, or hacks for growing in patience?

Devotions

Come to me, all you who labor and are burdened, and I will give you rest. Take my yoke upon you and learn of me, for I am meek and humble of heart; and you will find rest for yourselves. For my yoke is easy, and my burden light. Matthew 11:28-30

Sometimes it is hard to know where to focus when we look at Jesus. Scripture contains so many stories about things He did and words He shared. Over the course of the past two thousand years, theologians and lay people alike have shared their interpretations of His life. We want to love as He loved, but we can become overwhelmed by all the information.

Taking a complex and significant concept such as the love of God, a topic which continues to start wars among countries and family members alike, and distilling it down to a simple idea is difficult. Over time, people developed what are commonly referred to as "devotions" in order to focus attention on one aspect of God's love. Various devotions now exist as people respond in faith to what is happening in the world around us.

In much the same way as an icon on your phone represents an app that you can open and access information, a Catholic devotion represents an avenue to approach God. There are many devotions promoted by the Catholic Church over the centuries, which have enabled people to understand deeper truths through their participation in a collective communal activity, primarily prayer.

The devotion to the Sacred Heart of Jesus was officially promoted by the Catholic Church in 1956. In his encyclical *On the Devotion to the Sacred Heart*, Pope Pius XII described the devotion which had already been recognized by people in the pews for centuries.[1]

In most cultures, the heart is the symbolic source of love. The devotion to the Sacred Heart of Jesus honors Jesus' human and divine heart as the source of the profound sacrificial love that bought our salvation. In his encyclical, Pope Pius reminds us that Christ, through shedding His precious Blood in the

---

1 Pope Pius XII. "Haurietis Aquas". *The Holy See.* May 15, 1956, w2.vatican.va/content/pius-xii/en/encyclicals/documents/hf_p-xii_enc_15051956_haurietis-aquas.html

crucifixion, restored our friendship with God[2] It is sometimes easy to dismiss Jesus as not fully human when we read about all of His miracles and focus solely on His Resurrection. The devotion to His Sacred Heart counterbalances this temptation, reminding us of the wound in Jesus' heart which allows our restoration.

This devotion fuses the divine love shared amongst the Trinity and the human love of Jesus which directed His daily action among the people He met. This same love is shared with us and allows us to participate in Jesus' ongoing work in our own communities and families.

It may seem unusual to look at an image and ponder Jesus' love. Yet, that is just what has helped many people over the years gain a deeper understanding of the immense love and compassion that Jesus has for each of us. Pope Pius wrote, "Nothing therefore prevents our adoring the Sacred Heart of Jesus Christ as having a part in and being the natural and expressive symbol of the abiding love with which the divine Redeemer is still on fire for mankind."[3]

Many saints had great devotions to the Sacred Heart of Jesus, including St. Catherine of Siena and St. Gertrude the Great. St. Margaret Mary Alacoque popularized the devotion to the Sacred Heart after receiving visions and messages from Jesus encouraging her to share His love with others through a devotion to His Sacred Heart. The image of the Sacred Heart contains the outline of a human heart, pierced by a lance (sometimes dripping blood), surrounded by a crown of thorns. There is a cross on top of the heart usually surrounded by flames of divine love.

Many prayers and practices are dedicated to the Sacred Heart including venerating the image, wearing medals with the image, praying certain prayers and attending Mass on the First Friday of each month.

---

2   Id. Paragraph 78

3   Id. Paragraph 85

Gratitude

> *When I started counting my blessings,*
> *my whole life turned around. Willie Nelson*

We often resist growing in patience because it is so uncomfortable. Consider being grateful for the instances which allow you to grow in patience thinking instead of the beauty which will come once this muscle is strengthened.

Name three things teaching you patience right now.

1.

2.

3.

Scripture

Wait eagerly for the Lord, and keep His way; He will raise
you up to inherit the earth. Psalm 37:34

The Angel Gabriel reminds us that Mary was full of God's grace. The same grace that filled Mary is available to you. The Holy Spirit wants to fill you, dedicate the time and attention necessary to tending your relationship with Jesus. Just as the Holy Spirit overshadowed Mary, so too, the Holy Spirit can overshadow you if you rest in Him. The Holy Spirit wants to dwell within your soul and ignite His flame of love within you. Listen to the Psalmist as they tell you to wait *eagerly* for the Lord.

It is hard to imagine what it must have felt like to be overshadowed by the Holy Spirit. To be so overcome that you are impregnated with the Savior of the world. I don't think that this infusion of love dissipated quickly or left Mary alone. She needed this supernatural assistance to accompany her in all of the hard times in the days ahead.

Imagine that the Holy Spirit, the love between God and Jesus, fills Mary with the same love described by St. Paul in his letter to the Corinthians. He wants to continuously infuse you with this same love so that you can share it with each person you meet.

Once ignited, this flame of love will propel you forward just as Mary was propelled and strengthened in her journey with Jesus.

Read Luke 1:26-38

1. In verse 32, Gabriel delivers the "Good News" from God and describes Jesus. What 5 things does Gabriel say about Jesus?

   A.

   B.

   C.

   D.

   E.

2. What practical question does Mary ask?

3. How did the Angel describe the manner in which Jesus was to be conceived?

4. In verse 35 a reason is given for this unique manner of conception, why was Jesus not conceived in the traditional way?

5. Mary uses a word to describe herself and her role in connection with God, what word does she use?

Read Acts 1:13-14

6. Following Jesus' Ascension, the Eleven apostles are gathered in the Upper Room where they had shared the Last Supper with Jesus. Who else was with them? (Note: the term brothers used in this verse is understood to mean cousins or extended family, not biological brothers.)

7. Do you remember these women? What were they doing?

8. Do you think Mary was sharing the five things you wrote in your answer to question 1?

9. Mary's presence in the Upper Room reveals her continued trust in the angel's message from God. What one phrase stands out most to you from Luke 1:32?

10. Would natural patience allow Mary to gather in the Upper Room and continue to believe the words of the angel? Did Mary need supernatural help to sustain her trust in God? Explain.

If you have 5 minutes, Pray:

Repeat these words each time your patience is tested.

Dear Jesus, fill me with Your patience. I want to love as You love.

If you have 10 minutes, Ponder:

The Magnificat. (Luke 1:46-55)

   The words that spring forth from a patient heart.

If you have 15 minutes, Act:

Fast from the Instant this week. What is one thing that you rely upon that is instant? If it is texting, consider calling (and leaving a message) or emailing. If it is fast food— cook.

Prayer Intentions

Four

Lingering With Love

In all these things we conquer overwhelmingly through
Him who loved us. Romans 8:37

Introduction

God wants to heal and transform you so that you can see Him face to face and enjoy His presence in heaven for all eternity. It is easy to lose sight of this truth and become impatient with Him, ourselves, and others. Without the hope of heaven and the patience to remain on the path leading there, we take the details of our lives into our own hands and leave God behind. Without God, we travel the rocky path of the road back to heaven at a huge disadvantage, overburdened by things we were never meant to carry. Thankfully, God is patient and He waits for us.

We know from a lifetime of personal experience that love develops and deepens over time. It is revealed through actions, conversations, and sacrifice. Over months and years as we remain in relationship with other people, we come to trust them. We reveal more of ourselves to them and allow them access to our hearts and souls. Love grows as time is dedicated to nurturing relationships. The bonds of love are forged and strengthened as you walk together through good and bad times. Since trust and love grow slowly, patience is necessary.

Love cannot be rushed; otherwise, it remains superficial and fleeting rather than developing into something substantial and everlasting. Unfortunately, there are more examples of superficial relationships, which masquerade as love in our world, making it very difficult to discover the true substance of love.

St. Paul teaches what it means to be members of the body of Christ by encouraging us to seek love above all things. (1 Corinthians 12:31) In his first letter to the Corinthians, he outlines the many qualities of love. The first word Paul uses to describe love is *patient*. (1 Corinthians 13:4)

If we are lacking in patience, we enter our relationships at a disadvantage. Fortunately, God is patient and is willing to share this gift with us if we make ourselves available to Him. We need to approach the throne of Grace with confidence in Him and His Unfailing Love rather than fear so that we can receive all that He wants to share.

To experience love, we need to grow in patience with ourselves, others, and God.

Patience With Myself.

Patience starts as a seed in our soul. Unless the seed breaks open, grows roots, a stem, and leaves, it is impossible for patience to blossom. The only way to grow in patience is to experience events, which require us to exhibit patience. Unfortunately, this is uncomfortable due to our addiction to the instant. Growth is tough and can feel like your soul is stretching into hard soil as it searches for water. Our growth in patience is stunted if we aren't willing to be uncomfortable.

We must tread lightly anticipating and even expecting that we are going to stumble and fall. I would even go so far as to say we should celebrate our stumbles rather than moan about them. We will lose control of our tongue and say things we regret in a tone, which does not reveal a patient demeanor. We will also attempt to wrest control of our lives from God. As beginners, we will be clumsy and awkward. We cannot be surprised by our failure and should even welcome it as we develop new skills.

Pursuing a life grounded in love, abiding with Christ, requires supernatural patience. Each stumble is another opportunity to call out to God for help. The grace of God pours into us whenever we ask. He wants to assist us in growing in patience and will soften the soil of our souls with His living water when we pray. Thankfully, He is the author and creator of patience and has an overabundance of patience to wait for us. He also shares this patience with us through His Holy Spirit.

Patience With Others.

As we grow in patience with ourselves, we are naturally more patient with others. Growing in patience with others means abandoning our high expectations and anticipating that others will push our buttons and get on our nerves. Things will take longer than we would like. Much will not be done to our satisfaction.

When we are impatient, we overpower others with our words, silence, or exasperation. We can't love what we are trying to change. As we release our expectations, we find it easier to remain calm and peaceful on the inside. The people we love will experience this shift in our demeanor and will be more receptive to what we have to say. As we are more patient with others, they will grow to trust us more fully and we can love them more authentically.

Patience With God.

Part of abiding with Jesus is having patience with Him and His timing. There are many times in my past when I was tempted to give up on God, especially when things did not go according to my schedule or unfold in the way that I wanted. Can you relate? Bad things happen in life and we can be tempted to throw up our hands and ask God why He has abandoned us. We are not alone in feeling this way, as we know, Jesus asked this very question as He hung from the cross. (Matthew 47:26)

God is not finished writing your story, nor is He finished constructing His Kingdom. Patience allows you to remain open to Him as you continue to ask your questions.

So how do we grow in patience when it is so very uncomfortable to stay still? Most of us would sign up for the instant fix in a heartbeat if we thought we could avoid what we consider wasted time. Yet, God designed the world in such a way that things take time to grow. Since love is patient, patience helps us grow in love. There are four places to look with love when you are seeking patience: Back, Around, Up, and At Other People.

Looking At Life Through The Eyes Of Love.

1. Look Back with Love

We know growth is slow and often imperceptible with the human eye. Measured day after day, not much happens. But, with the perspective of time, growth is noticeable and often remarkable.

Think of the little girl you have not seen in several years and then you run into her at church or the grocery store. The last time you saw her you were driving her to soccer practice, now she is driving alone. You notice everything that is different about her, things that her mother takes for granted, and does not see. Her physical growth took years, but to you it seems as though it was the blink of an eye.

Reflection on the past is needed to recognize how far you have come and how much you have grown. Some of us don't look back because of the pain associated with certain memories or personal failures; therefore, we face forward and diminish our own potential positive impact on the world failing to learn from our past. When our eyes are fixed firmly on rushing toward the future, we forget where we have been. Pausing to see how far you have come and celebrating the journey is important. Looking on our past with eyes of love and forgiveness is crucial if we want to abide with Christ in the future.

2. Look Around
Sometimes we lack patience with our circumstances and take this out on other people. In order to grow in patience, we need to know which relationships or circumstances need tilling. Identify the instances that try your patience. Look around and see what causes you to lose your temper (or possibly what caused you to retreat inside yourself) over the span of a few days. When you flare up or retreat away from people, you are unable to actively love them.

Looking around will help you recognize patterns in your own life. It may be that certain people test your patience and you need to prayerfully prepare yourself to interact with them. On the other hand, that irritation may be rooted in lack of sleep, too much junk food, or not enough exercise. You won't know unless you look back with love.

3. Look Up
Gazing upon God in prayerful gratitude, making a note of all of the things that are going right in your day, week, or year is another great practice. Once you begin to notice all that is beautiful in your day, you will find it difficult to rush through life when there are so many great things to savor in the present moment.

Return your mind to the hope of heaven and the promise of eternal life. God works at a slow pace where we often fail to recognize His presence when we are not paying attention. The same thing is true about our spiritual life. If we are nourishing our soul with prayer, the Mass, the Sacraments, reflection on Scripture, and service to others, we will experience growth and can trust that God is at work even if we do not feel like anything is happening.

4. Look at Others with Love

If you are honest, there is at least one person who gets on your nerves. You can expand your capacity to love by reframing your thoughts about interactions with those you love but who mostly try your patience. Changing your mindset about what is irritating and turning that quality into something that is endearing will allow you to grow in patience with her rather than gritting your teeth.

First, name one thing that irritates you most about them. For instance, she may have the annoying habit of saying OK at the end of every statement. When you are with her, every conversation becomes a white knuckle experience as you begin to count the number of OK's she says. Listening through ears of impatience, you might not be able to make it through three or four exchanges before you break down and say something you regret.

Imagine what would happen if, before you talk to her, you reframe the way you hear this conversational tick. Could you listen and think how wonderful it is that she is unique and no-one else on the planet has this same vocal thumbprint? Looking with eyes of love and listening with ears of love helps you visit without losing your temper.

Hope in the power of the unfailing love of God fuels our patient pursuit of Jesus. Patience and hope walk hand in hand. Just as Mary and the apostles waited with patience and hope for the Holy Spirit at Pentecost, we too must wait with hope for the fulfillment of God's promise: that His Kingdom will not end. God's love endures and will never fail. An increase in patience expands our capacity to abide in God's love.

Questions

1. Mary uses a unique term to describe herself when she accepts her role as the mother of God. She calls herself a handmaiden. For a handmaiden to be successful, patience is a key quality. It allows her to notice and respond to needs of others. We can't serve others if we are constantly focused on our own irritation in the present or barreling forward toward the future.

2. Why is it important to be patient with yourself?

3. Why should we be patient with other people?

4. What can happen if we are patient with God?

5. What does patience with God look like in every day life?

6. It is important to look at life through the eyes of love. Which one way of "looking" at your life with love would you like to try: back, around, up, or at others? Why?

7. What is one thing you can do this week that will allow you to Look with Love?

8. Last week we read about the impact that instant everything is having on our outlook. What is one instant thing that you can take a break from in order to strengthen your patience muscle?

9. "Impatience is an impediment to accepting the love of God which heals." Where do you find impatience popping up in your life?

Women of Faith

Commit your way to the Lord; trust in Him and He will act. Psalm 37:3

For centuries women religious have written their spiritual inspirations down in the hopes of helping other women in their midst encounter Jesus and understand what it means to abide with Him. St. Faustina (d.1938) received messages from Jesus in prayer and maintained a diary which is available today. St. Teresa Benedicta of the Cross (d. 1942) was an intellectual Jewish convert turned religious sister who died at the hands of the Nazis. St. Katherine Drexel (d. 1955), the first American born saint, started an order focused primarily on educating African American and Native American children. The wisdom possessed by these women continues to inspire today.

"In difficult moments I will fix my gaze upon the silent heart of Jesus, stretched upon the cross, and from the exploding flames of His merciful Heart, will flow down upon me power and strength to keep fighting." St. Faustina

"God is there in these moments of rest and can give us in a single instant exactly what we need. Then the rest of the day can take its course, under the same effort and strain, perhaps, but in peace. And when night comes, and you look back over the day and see how fragmentary everything has been, and how much you planned that has gone undone, and all the reasons you have to be embarrassed and ashamed: just take everything exactly as it is, put it in God's hands and leave it with Him. Then you will be able to rest in Him — really rest — and start the next day as a new life." St. Teresa Benedicta of the Cross (Edith Stein)

"Peacefully do at each moment what at that moment ought to be done. If we do what each moment requires, we will eventually complete God's plan, whatever it is. We can trust God to take care of the master plan when we take care of the details." St. Katharine Drexel

Scripture

The Lord, your God, is in your midst,a mighty savior,
Who will rejoice over you with gladness,and renew you in his love,
Who will sing joyfully because of you.
Zephaniah 3:17

Depending upon where today finds you, our first Scripture passage you read may stir your soul and encourage you to hug the nearest person you can find.

On the other hand, the words may be heartbreaking. If you are in a season of struggle, this passage might cause you to want to run and hide at the thought of all the times when you have experienced the pain that comes when love is neither patient nor kind. If this passage is one that brings tears of pain and sorrow to you eyes, I hope that you will have the courage to leave behind your memories of times when love has failed.

Turn your heart instead toward the One whose love never fails. Look forward with hope knowing that Jesus is all that St. Paul describes, and more. You have everything you need to join Jesus on the journey of love. You are enough, you have enough, come as you are and invite Him along.

We often think St. Paul, in 1 Corinthians, is pointing out how we are to act toward others. That is true. Yet, his words point to another fundamental truth—one that is often overlooked by us as we read this popular passage. In describing love, St. Paul gives us a list of qualities, outlining God's essential nature and by extension Jesus, His Son.

Read 1 Corinthians 13:1-13

1. We know from St. John that *God is love* (1 John 4:16). Read verses 4-8 and substitute the name Jesus for the word love. Which aspect of Jesus's nature did you stumble over, thinking that it did not align with your vision of Him?

2. This passage may be one of the most familiar in the entire Bible. What strikes you most as you read it today?

3. It is easy to fool ourselves into believing that there are many things more important to our spiritual growth than love itself. We look for spiritual gifts and marvel in miracles. We busy ourselves with volunteer work and reading mountains of books. Yet, St. Paul says that the spiritual gifts, martyrdom, and prophetic utterances are only a partial glimpse of God's reality. These things alone are not enough to reveal God to the world. What must be present in combination with each of these things?

4. In verse 12, St. Paul talks about seeing someone face to face. Who is that someone and when will this happen?

5. Do we fully understand God or ourselves today? To what does Paul equate our obscured vision?

Read 1 John 4:7-21

6. Who are we to love?

7. Why should we love other people?

8. Do we love on our own or as a result of supernatural help?

9. Does St. John believe in the continued presence and action of God on earth? What verses support your answer?

10. How was the love of God revealed to us?

Read Acts 16:11-15, 40

11. Why do you think Paul talks to the women? What do you think their conversation was like?

12. What is Lydia's profession? Do you get the impression she is successful?

13. What does she ask of Paul? Why do you think she asked this?

14. Do you get the impression that Lydia eventually gathers more followers for Christ? Why or why not?

15. It is risky during this time to profess your belief in Jesus, what do you think Lydia saw and heard in Paul and the disciples which made her willing to risk it all to experience the love of Jesus?

16. What role does love play in drawing Paul back to Lydia's house?

Putting It Into Practice

If you have 5 minutes, Pray:
Notice each time that you have to wait this week.
    Each time, pray:

> *Dear God, give me Your supernatural patience,*
> *help me to see You in my waiting.*
> *Amen.*

If you have 10 minutes, Ponder:
What does it mean for the Kingdom of God to have no end? Does this give you hope as you seek to bring more love into the world as an ambassador of God?

Or

St. Paul calls us to put on the love of God when we interact with other people. Time, attention, and forgiveness are three of the many building blocks of a relationship. Love is the mortar that binds it together. Is love the mortar of your life or is something else holding it all together?

If you have 15 minutes, Act:
Call a friend you have not spoken to in a long time. It might be someone with whom you can reflect about how you have grown and changed in recent years. Maybe it is a friend you need to encourage. Or, it is someone who pushes your buttons a little and with whom you need to exercise patience.

Prayer Intentions

_____

_____

_____

_____

_____

_____

_____

_____

_____

_____

_____

_____

_____

_____

_____

_____

_____

_____

_____

_____

_____

Five

Submitting to Merciful Love

Jesus, make me a saint according to Your own heart, meek and humble. St. Mother Teresa of Calcutta

Introduction

There is a great debate in my house over which is the better problem solver: Neosporin or the Dust Buster. Silly, but true. Whenever anyone has a cut or scrape, my husband becomes the Neosporin bully following you around the house insisting that you apply and reapply in the hopes that you will heal without a scar.

I am not as devoted to Neosporin as my husband; my allegiance is to something completely different. My favorite way to fix a problem is to head for the Dust Buster. If there is a spill or extra dog fur, I am forever asking a child to get the Dust Buster out to vacuum up the mess. I have an indefatigable trust in the power of the Dust Buster to suck up anything you do not want the guests to see.

Both Neosporin and the Dust Buster make your problem virtually disappear as if it never existed.

While I am a die-hard Dust Buster fan, I have to give the crown to Neosporin as the better problem solver, though. Neosporin contains properties, which activate the body's immune system encouraging healing and preventing infection. In the long run that is probably more important than something that cleans at the surface level.

We each have things in life we regret. Usually, the little things weigh most heavily on our minds. It might be the way we talked to our husband, our mother, or our child. Or the number of people we cut off in traffic when we were in a rush. In order to quell our inner angst, we often look for ways to fix our messes and make ourselves feel better.

In the same way I pull out the Dust Buster to get rid of my dust bunnies, I might pop into Starbucks or Target for a quick emotional fix to help mask my issues in the short term. (It's even better if the Target has a Starbucks!) Your quick fix might be exercise, a piece of chocolate, planning a vacation or dreaming about a new kitchen. These remedies, while a great distraction, are superficial and surface level. The quick fix is never going to solve the real problem.

What we really need is a solution that goes deeper, rooting out the problem instead of applying a Band-Aid and hoping the problem will just go away once it is out of sight or out of mind. The solution must work from the inside out and enable us to respond differently in the future. We need a salve that can reach deep inside our souls and mend our most hidden wounds: a healing power that can gently restore the innocence that has been lost.

God's love is the only antidote to heal the wounds left from our encounters with others. Jesus is the One who can soothe the pain caused by our and other people's sin. Abiding with Him is the beginning of the healing process. But first, we need to be willing to submit ourselves to Him.

Our souls are greatly affected by a lifetime of experiences. The positive experiences encourage us toward virtue and exercising self-giving love. Unfortunately, we also encounter negative events, which try our patience and tempt us to react in ways that create wedges between ourselves and other people.

The resistance to exhibiting and receiving love, otherwise known as sin, affects us in many ways we don't always recognize. Sin damages us from the inside out. When we see sin as something to be vacuumed up or swept under the rug, we misunderstand its very nature, thinking our actions are merely temporary without any lasting effect. In reality, sin leaves cuts, bruises, and scrapes in the fabric of our souls, families, and communities. Ignored and unaddressed, the wounds impact our daily lives and our relationships.

Any time we make a *conscious* choice that is contrary to love, we sin. (*see* CCC 1846-1876) This includes what we do and what we chose not to do, the sins of commission and omission. Remember, for something to be a sin, we need to know that the behavior is wrong or contrary to God's design. In order to recognize when our action or inaction is contrary to love, our consciences need to become more sensitive to God's voice.

How we view sin will determine whether we take it to the foot of the cross and leave it there or put it in our designer bag and hide it from Jesus. We don't like to admit our weakness and failures. Sin has become the word that must not be mentioned. In fact, it is probably more acceptable to say some four-letter words today rather than whisper the word *sin* at all. Our unwillingness to talk about sin causes us to misunderstand its effects on our bodies and souls contributing to our inability to identify the cure.

God's mercy is the antidote to sin. Much of our sin comes from a failure to understand God's true nature. As St. Paul wrote, love does not rejoice over the wrongdoings of others, but rejoices in the truth. (1 Corinthians 13:6) So, it follows, God does not rejoice in our wrongdoing.

When we misunderstand God's love and His true nature, we are unable to abide with Him.

If we mistakenly believe that God gets excited about our sin so that He can step in to correct us, we will assign Him the role of the *Authority*. Here, we think that He is waiting to smack us down any time we step out of line. We are afraid of Him and fail to approach Him, anxious about how He is going to punish us. We aren't sure what the punishment will be, so we hide parts of ourselves in fear. It is difficult to imagine resting in the presence of this image of God; instead, we imagine ourselves cowering in a corner, our faces buried in our knees.

On other days, we are equally mistaken to believe that God is the *Indulger* and does not care about our choices at all. Many believe God is so indulgent that He will give us all that we want regardless of whether our desires are in our soul's best interest or good for the community as a whole. When our focus is primarily on ourselves, we pursue what we think will make us happy in the short term disregarding the negative impact on the people around us. This belief disregards the second half of the verse where St. Paul writes that God rejoices in the truth.

We vacillate between these two views of God often without realizing it. At either end, God's mercy is unnecessary because we place ourselves on the throne of our hearts and crown ourselves queen without the need for a king.

Mercy is one of the key qualities of God's love. As such, we can be confident that God is neither the Authority nor the Indulger.

As we abide with Jesus, we spend more time in the middle ground where God's justice and merciful love dwell.

Calling out for God's Mercy.

Quite often, it is not until we face a huge life hurdle and are hanging on to the last knot in our rope that we call out to God for help. This is a difficult place to be because we are not experienced in asking for help for ourselves. We are used to interceding for others, believing God will hear our prayers in those instances. But, for some reason, we most often neglect the needs of our own souls when we pray. So, when what was working in the past no longer succeeds, we must begin to recognize that God's mercy is vital to the health of our soul and ask for His help before we reach the end of our rope.

The Woman Caught in Adultery was seeking love, but not from the right person. The men in power used her as a pawn, and she was powerless to save her own life. Despite her utter powerlessness, she remained in the presence of Mercy and silently waited to see what would happen. She knew that she had nowhere else to go and so did Jesus.

So, what does Jesus do? He hands her a new rope. One tied to Him. Jesus, in His gentle, silent way helped her recognize that God saw and loved her. She had His full attention. Jesus knew what drew her to her adulterous behavior and He loved her. He did not hold a scorecard reading off her infractions. He did not give her a pass either. No, He forgave her. Her sin was still a sin, but His mercy prevailed.

In much the same way, our Catholic faith hands us a lifeline in the form of Confession. This healing sacrament is similar to placing Neosporin on a wound, healing your soul. There is nothing you have done He will not forgive. There is no choice, no action you have taken which is an impediment to the power of His love. When you submit to His merciful love, confess your sins, and let go of the burden of past sins, you experience a peace and joy unlike anything else available. With His peace, you can then begin to see how truly important it is to extend forgiveness to others and are empowered to do so by His grace.

Questions

1. How do our quick fixes distract us from the one thing, which will heal our soul?

2. What is sin?

3. What happens when we fail to recognize what is a sin and what is merely a mistake or an accident?

4. What healing sacrament helps you to let go of the burden of past sins and experience healing?

5. What is the danger in seeing God as "The Authority"? What happens when we think that God celebrates our mistakes and sins?

6. What is the danger in seeing God as "The Indulger"? What happens when we think that God is not concerned about the truth or sin?

7. Why do we avoid going to Confession?

Gratitude

Find your delight in the Lord Who will give
you your heart's desire. Psalm 37:4

As we delight ourselves in the Lord, it is harder to look critically at ourselves and other people. Name three times you are grateful God gave you the grace to forgive another person. Alternatively, name three things delighting you lately.

1.

2.

3.

Scripture

His mercy is from age to age for those who fear Him. Luke 1:30

In John 7, the Pharisees and the chief priests order guards to arrest Jesus. Instead of arresting Him, they are amazed at Jesus' teaching. So the scribes and Pharisees decide to take matters in their own hands and set a trap for Jesus in John 8.

The Pharisees and scribes see God as "The Authority", He is tough and hard nosed because people need to be kept in line, punishing every violation of His rigid rules. From this point of view, all of God's attention is intended to teach lessons and punish infractions. All rules come from the top and are not meant to be questioned or challenged, merely followed to the letter. God, in this viewpoint, is all-powerful and reveals His power through punishment. This is not the true "fear of the Lord" Mary references in the Magnificat when she declares that His mercy lasts from age to age. (Luke 1:46-55)

People holding this point of view are afraid of God's attention because of their uncertainty about His potential punishment. So they follow the rules as they are written without looking to the purpose behind the rule. Love does not factor into the equation because rigidity keep bad people in line better than any other method. In this view, sin is held in check by firm rules and harsh punishment. One danger in seeing God as a harsh taskmaster looking to admonish us for every toe we step out of line is that our human nature turns that same imaginary measuring stick against others.

Not even realizing it, we may view God as the Authority and ourselves as part of His enforcement team. Our natural desire to get ahead in life can encourage us to silently clap when we see someone else fail to live up to our own high standards which we mistake as God's high standards. As their bad choices knock them down a peg in our imagination, our good choices move us to a higher standing. We are tempted to silently pat ourselves on the back as we compare and think we are walking on the narrow path while others wander in the wilderness. In this case, we take control from the Just Judge (God) and pass judgment ourselves. This mindset is completely contrary to the merciful love of God. (*See* Matthew 7:1-5)

There are multiple dangers with this mindset. When we are judgmental, we have a tendency of failing to acknowledge or even hide our own sins. We do not want to be considered like "those other people" we have mistakenly judged so harshly. This skewed mindset is an enormous obstacle to abiding with Jesus.

The Woman Caught in Adultery might view God as "The Indulger" before she meets Jesus. She possibly lives on the edge of acceptability, flaunting the rules, not concerned about the potential punishment because she has not seen others punished for the same behavior. Thinking that God overlooks everything, she thinks the Ten Commandments and Levitical Laws are merely suggestions to follow. She might believe God just wants her to have fun and enjoy all that life has to offer, no matter how her behavior affects other people. The rules don't really matter as long as no one is hurt too badly. Sin doesn't really exist because what she is doing has no long-term effects.

In this view, even if someone sins, there is no need for forgiveness, repentance, and there is no punishment because "The Indulger" just wants *you* to be happy in the short term. God, in this view, is similar to the lenient parents whose sole mission is to be friends with their child and indulges that child's every whim. In this case, God is easily dismissed as irrelevant because He lacks authority and power. If you believe God is the Indulger, you don't need His mercy because there is no sin.

The beauty of our Scripture passage reveals an alternative. God, in the person of Jesus, reveals Himself to be God "The Merciful", the One in whom it is so easy to delight. Jesus does not deny the existence of sin, nor does He condemn the woman for her sin. No, Jesus welcomes her. As you read, pray, and ponder our passages this week, ask the Holy Spirit to help you recognize how a Merciful God differs from The Authority and The Indulger. Ask Him to open your heart to delight in His mercy.

Read John 8:1-11

1. After spending a night alone in prayer what causes Jesus to sit down
    and start teaching?

2. Read Deuteronomy 22:22. Who should be punished if they are caught
    in adultery? What do the officials say is the law (John 8:5)?

3. Do the Pharisees and scribes accurately depict the law?

4. What is the first thing Jesus says?

5. Who leaves first? Why do you think they were the first to go?

6. Who was the only one at the scene without sin?

7. Did the woman have an opportunity to leave? Why do you think she remains?

8. What did Jesus tell her?

9. What do you think that the woman caught in adultery was thinking when Jesus looked at her and spoke? What changed in her?

10. Does Jesus speak differently to the people in power compared to the way he speaks to the women? (See Luke 13:15-17 and John 8:7)

11. Where are you in the story of the Woman caught in Adultery? Are you judging, are you being judged, or are you the silent bystander who walks away without defending the woman because you do not want to get involved?

12. The woman caught in adultery abides with Jesus. What are some other words that you could use in this sentence to replace the word abide? What are synonyms for abide?

13. There is something striking in the different way that the Pharisees and the woman respond to Jesus. What is the difference between the way the Pharisees respond to Jesus and the way the woman responds?

If you have 5 minutes, Pray:

St. Catherine of Siena was devoted to the Sacred Heart of Jesus to such an extraordinary degree that she spiritually exchanged her heart for that of Jesus' heart. We can do the same thing today by offering the prayer used by St. Catherine of Siena. Delight yourself in Him and trust that He has your best interest in mind.

O most holy Heart of Jesus, fountain of every blessing, I adore You, I love You and will a lively sorrow for my sins. I offer You this poor heart of mine. Make me humble, patient, pure, and wholly obedient to Your will. Grant, good Jesus, that I may live in You and for You. Protect me in the midst of danger; comfort me in my afflictions; give me health of body, assistance in my temporal needs, Your blessings on all that I do, and the grace of a holy death. Within Your heart I place my every care. In every need let me come to You with humble trust saying, Heart of Jesus, help me. Amen

If you have 10 minutes, Ponder:

Who do I judge? Is it myself or others? Am I willing to release this job to the Just Judge?

If you have 15 minutes, Act:

Spend 15 minutes in Adoration whether in Church or in nature. Delight yourself in Jesus and ask Him to show you how He is delighted with you.

Prayer Intentions

_____

_____

_____

_____

_____

_____

_____

_____

_____

_____

_____

_____

_____

_____

_____

_____

_____

_____

_____

_____

_____

_____

Six

Experiencing Peace

*I strive for silence in my heart amidst the greatest sufferings, and
I protect myself against all attacks with the shield of Your Name.
St. Faustina (Diary entry 1040)*

Introduction

Part of learning to rest with Jesus is embracing all that He has to offer. One of the most beautiful aspects of His love is revealed in His mercy. Yet, we often run away from Him rather than toward Him when we are most in need of His restorative love.

Mercy is profoundly difficult to understand when we struggle to truly forgive and see little evidence of this beautiful trait in other people. It is hard to fathom limitless forgiveness, a love that restores rather than rebukes. If we are to be women who are able to receive and give love like Jesus, we must come to understand the relationship between our sin and God's mercy in a new way.

Our relationship with God is triangulated including not only ourselves and God, but other people as well. The health of our relationship with God includes how we treat other people. In the Sermon on the Mount, Jesus gives us many teachings about how this triangulated relationship should look. Many of the admonitions seem outlandish and impossible. Love your enemies and pray for those who persecute you. (Matthew 5:44) Stop judging. (Matthew 7:1) If you forgive others their transgressions, your heavenly Father will forgive you. (Matthew 6:14) We want to love and follow Jesus' teachings, unfortunately we are generous with our judgments and stingy with our forgiveness.

It is hard to face our weaknesses, our missteps, and our failures to resist temptation. While it is easy for me to reflexively say, "I am sorry" for stepping on someone's toe, it is harder to apologize for running over someone with my negative words. It is embarrassing to admit that I am judgmental and selfish. Sadly, in an effort to avoid the short term pain of suffering a paper cut to my pride and admit I am wrong to myself and the person I have injured, I allow my sins to go unexamined. Going too long without a good reflection, my soul suffers as I reject an opportunity to ask for and accept God's mercy.

Instead of forgiving, we keep score. Many of us maintain a card catalogue full of grievances. Filed away, they eventually morph into bitterness and anger. Sadly, our failure to forgive others and ourselves affects not only our soul, but also our health. Our ability to cling tightly to resentment negatively impacts our relationship with God, ourselves, and other people. Pushing our feelings of guilt away, we allow our hearts to harden, our blood pressure to soar, and our arteries to clog as our unresolved sin infects our souls and divides relationships. We become so comfortable with our patterns of thinking that we wrap ourselves in the security blanket of shame instead of resting in His embrace, not realizing how cumbersome this shame becomes over time.

Sin Divides—Mercy Restores

If your internal monologue is not driving you to Jesus, it is time to replace the scripts of the recording. What negative words are on repeat in your mind? When your mind is occupied with condemnation, you are too distracted to seek God's love. Complacency sets in as you believe nothing will ever change. You become tempted to give yourself a pass on the harder passages you read in the Gospels thinking they are for people whose life is a bit easier than your own.

The words we have on repeat in our minds need to be filled with the Word of Jesus so that He may dwell even more comfortably in our hearts. As we condemn others and ourselves for past mistakes, we chip away at the Kingdom of God, making it more difficult for Him to find a welcome place to rest.

We don't want to wake up every day as criticizers and condemners, but this is what happens when we fail to accept God's mercy. You have the choice today. Hide in the shadows of shame or step out and become a Kingdom builder and peace bearer.

Imperfection Is An Invitation From God

While it is important for us to acknowledge our misbehaviors, our sins, it is even more important for us to see that our imperfections are an invitation from God. If we were perfect, we would not need Jesus. Our imperfections are exactly why Jesus was born. His mercy restores what we, in our own power, are unable to heal.

God's mercy is available to each and every one of us. The only sin that can't be forgiven is the one we don't take to Jesus. What our actions separate, God mends. As we accept His forgiveness, this beautiful mercy of Jesus, our souls begin to heal. His healing allows us to release the bitterness, which has built up over many years, and helps us to begin extending heartfelt forgiveness to those around us.

His mercy moves us to tears and drives us to Jesus' feet where we can pour our hearts out to Him. Once empty, He can fill our hearts with His love and peace. God's mercy lightens the burdens on our bodies and our souls allowing us to become more present to everyone around us and recognize their needs. Our critical eye transforms into the eye of affirmation.

Jesus does not condemn you for your sin when you approach Him; He forgives. He sees you and knows you. He accepts you as you are and wants to restore you to the woman He originally crafted in love. It is vital to recognize that any words of condemnation that are on repeat in your head are not the voice of Jesus; they are not His Word.

Jesus exhibited mercy to many of the people He met as He walked, healed, and taught. He sought to restore people not only to physical health, but to spiritual health as well. *Those who are healthy do not need a physician, but the sick do. I have not come to call the righteous to repentance but sinners.* (Luke 5:31) Mercy seeks to reunite what sin has divided. If we hold on to the belief that we are not sinners in need of mercy, we miss out on intimate conversations with Jesus.

There is a beautiful exchange that only Jesus makes possible. He takes our sins, if we are willing to let them go. In exchange, He gives us His peace. It is time to look into the eyes of Jesus as He speaks His healing words to you. Internalize Jesus' powerful words, *Peace I leave with you. My peace I give to you. Not as the world gives do I give it to you.* (John 14:27) Jesus knows that your burdens are too heavy to carry alone. He wants to give you the confidence to walk away from shame so that you are free to rise up and go with Him. (John 14:31)

Questions

1. Many of us are hiding under a security blanket of shame. What happens in people's lives to cause them to weave a blanket of protection around themselves?

2. We are stifled by fear of condemnation, afraid of what others will say. What part of life do we opt out of for fear of condemnation?

3. We are held fast by the bonds of bitterness. Do you struggle to forgive yourself or others?

4. What are the barriers to forgiveness in your life?

5. Why is it easier to repeat words of condemnation to ourselves over silly, petty little things rather than speak words of mercy and love to ourselves?

6. What stops you from remaining with Jesus and hearing His words of forgiveness?

7. How is imperfection an invitation from God?

8. If you were perfect, would you need Jesus?

Women of Faith

The Lord is gracious and merciful, slow to anger
and abounding in mercy. Psalm 145:8

St. Faustina was a simple nun who died of tuberculosis at in 1938 in Krakow, Poland at the age of 33. Born to a poor family, she had to leave home to become a housekeeper in order to support herself. She tried to enter several different convents, but was rejected due to her precarious health. In prayer, Jesus directed her to the convent which eventually accepted her. She entered the convent and maintained a deep union with Christ in prayer. Jesus revealed much to her, which she recorded in her diary.

Faustina received very little education so she was assigned the most menial tasks either in the kitchen or garden. She never held a position of power or prestige, yet she maintained a very intimate relationship with Jesus and was chosen by Him to communicate a very important message to a world broken by war.

The heart of her spirituality is based in the Divine Mercy of God. Jesus asked that she have the Divine Mercy image painted and wanted her to encourage everyone to trust in Him. Because St. Faustina abided with Jesus, we have the devotion to Divine Mercy which is celebrated on the first Sunday after Easter.

Mercy is the flower of love. God is love, and mercy is His deed. In love it is conceived; in mercy it is revealed. Everything I look at speaks to me of God's mercy. Even God's very justice speaks to me about His fathomless mercy, because justice flows from love. Diary, 651.

St. Faustina wrote often of the need to pray on behalf of the sick and the dying that they may experience the full mercy of God.

I realize more and more how much every soul needs God's mercy throughout life and particularly at the hour of death. Diary, 1036

She reminds us of the power of God's love to forgive and restore, if we but just ask.

Even if I had the sins of the whole world, as well as the sins of all the condemned souls weighing on my conscience, I would not have doubted God's goodness but, without hesitation, would have thrown myself into the abyss of The Divine Mercy, which is always open to us; and, with a heart crushed to dust, I would cast myself at His feet, abandoning myself totally to His holy will, which is mercy itself. Diary, 1552

If there is any encouragement in Christ, any solace in love, any participation in the Spirit, any compassion and mercy, complete my joy by being of the same mind, with the same love, united in heart, thinking one thing. Philippians 2:1-2

As we read earlier, most people in Jesus' day kept Him at arm's length. In our Scripture this week, we will find two people with vastly different reactions to Jesus. Their attitudes were driven by their own internal monologue. The Pharisee saw Jesus as one teacher among many; the sinful woman understood His merciful love and knew He was the One. Their internal dispositions determined their actions.

Read Luke 7: 36-50

1. Who does the Pharisee judge and why?

2. What does the woman do for Jesus?

3. Do you think this woman encountered Jesus before this dinner or had she merely only heard about Him from other people?

4. Jesus acknowledges the existence of sin in this passage. When do you think this woman's sins were forgiven, before the dinner or during the dinner? Why?

5. Who does Jesus say shows great love?

6. What does Jesus tell the woman before she leaves? What does this mean to you?

7. Do we have to present ourselves or make ourselves available to Jesus in order to take advantage of God's merciful love and for our sins to be forgiven?

Our next passage is part of the Last Supper Discourse where Jesus is telling his closest friends what they can expect and how He wants them to live going forward. Much of what He says twists and turns.

Read John 14:15-31

8. What will we do if we love Jesus?

9. Who will love us if we love Jesus?

10. What happens if we love Jesus?

11. What role does the Holy Spirit play in helping us keep Jesus' word?

12. What does Jesus leave with His disciples?

13. What are the final words of this passage? Why do you think Jesus says this?

14. What does this passage mean to you in light of all that we have studied so far?

Putting it into Practice

If you have 5 minutes, Pray:

*O my God, Trinity whom I adore, help me to forget myself entirely that
I may be established in You, as still and as peaceful as if my soul were
already in eternity. Give peace to my soul; make it Your heaven. Amen.*
St. Elizabeth of the Trinity

If you have 10 minutes, Ponder:

*The valiant one whose steps are guided by the Lord,
who will delight in His way, may stumble, but he will never
fall, for the Lord holds his hand.*
Psalm 37:23-24

Jesus wants you to look Him in the eye and hear the words, "I do not condemn you." He wants for you to stop condemning yourself and enter His embrace. With Him, you are filled with His peace and empowered to avoid sin.

If you have 15 minutes, Act:
Accept the mercy of Jesus. Imagine you are present when the adulterous woman is brought to the temple area. You have been listening to Jesus teach and are mesmerized by His insights. There is a commotion and you see several scribes and Pharisees dragging a woman to Jesus. Instead of condemning the woman, the scribes and Pharisees turn to you.

Imagine that each scribe is a critic reminding you of all the ways you do not measure up, he names each of the mistakes you have made. What do they have to say? What does Jesus say?

Next, imagine the Pharisees. Each of them is a critic to remind you of each rule and commandment you ever broke. What do they have to say?

Look to Jesus. What does He have to say?

Now that all of the dirty laundry is out on the line, look into His eyes of love and let His mercy wash over you. Jesus speaks to you and says, "I love you. I do not condemn you. I came for you. I am here to restore you and heal you. My peace I leave with you"

Ask Him to reveal the lies you are believing, which prevent you from abiding in His love.

Prayer Intentions

_____

_____

_____

_____

_____

_____

_____

_____

_____

_____

_____

_____

_____

_____

_____

_____

_____

_____

_____

_____

Seven

Pursued by Love

Rejoice in hope, endure in affliction, preserve in prayer. Romans 12:12

*Give yourself fully to Jesus, He will use you to accomplish great
things on the condition that you believe much more in
His Love than in your weakness.
St. Mother Teresa of Calcutta*

Introduction

Several years ago we adopted a Catholic dog, crazy, I know. For the better part of my life I have had many different breeds of dogs. Over the years there were a few cats sprinkled in the mix, but for the most part we are a dog family. It was not until this little Labradoodle came into my life that I realized that dogs could nestle into a place deep in your heart.

After graduating from college, looking to normalize my otherwise chaotic life, I got a dog and experienced my first taste of parenting failure. (Yes, I realize that I was not truly parenting, but the dog was good practice for the children I later parented.) I would love to wax eloquently about how this dog and I were not a good fit, but at the end of the day, a Brittany Spaniel is not happy in a one bedroom apartment with a law student. That poor dog was yet another thing I chased after which did not bring the calm and peace to my life that I was so sorely missing.

Which brings me to the dog that we currently own, the Catholic one. Now that I have ample time on my hands, Maggie and I spend lots of time together. The children have flown the coop and are making their own way into their young adult lives, so I have a greater appreciation for Maggie's company. She is here to listen which allows me to feel as though I am not talking to myself. She walks with me every day and is a great conduit for conversation with my neighbors. While she often barks at nothing, I feel safer with her as she sounds ferocious.

I am the only one who feeds her, so she follows me around the house moving from one room to the next as I go about my day. She is persistent in making her requests known whether it is to be fed or to go outside to chase the birds. Maggie is protective and does not like to be separated from me. When I am not home, she gets into mischief, which is how I know her religious affiliation.

While other dogs in my life have been dedicated to chewing shoes, Maggie is dedicated to Jesus. Many days when I get home, I discover that she has found a book and put it in the middle of my bed. Often, there are bite marks on the cover or a few pages missing that she enjoyed eating. Inevitably, the books are written by Catholic authors and quite often have been books about Mary. While I am sad to have damaged books, I think that the Holy Spirit works through her to call my attention back to what really matters in life.

Do you have a deep dedication to your pet? Whether you are a dog, cat, or reptile person, you too may have discovered how animals are persistent in getting their needs met.

In the next Scripture passage you will read, you will find the Canaanite woman who is seeking healing for her daughter. At first, you might be shocked when Jesus compares the Canaanite woman to a dog and wonder how Jesus can talk to her that way and not risk being slapped. I mean who wants to be compared to a dog? Especially if you think stray dogs or mongrels are the category of animal that Jesus is referring to.

Yet, she does not respond negatively. The Canaanite woman speaks directly and with persistence. She is not offended, nor is she taking no for an answer, she believes that Jesus is the One to help her daughter. This woman is brilliant in the way she banters with Jesus, taking His statement and turning it on its head. She is persistent in her belief and takes their conversation one step further.

Dogs are shameless in their adoration of their chosen person. They pursue that person, wandering from room to room until they can finally settle at the feet of the one they love. They beg, snuggle, wag their tails in joy, they reveal their hearts without a filter. They are calm when they are close to their people and anxious when separated. Dogs love wholeheartedly and can teach us a thing or two about what it means to love.

You are always pursued by Jesus, who wants to pour out His unfailing love from His Sacred Heart and lavish you with His grace.

We often don't consider being the object of another's pursuit once we have reached a certain age and allowed our romantic imaginations to fade under the bright light of reality. Yet, the poet Francis Thompson refers to Jesus as the "hound of heaven". This poem, beloved by G.K. Chesterton and J.R.R. Tolkien, tells the story of a man who is pursued by Love just as a hound pursues a rabbit. The man is afraid so he runs to any distraction imaginable while Love follows behind patiently waiting for the man to turn around.

Interestingly, Jesus' pursuit often feels like waves on the ocean, hitting us then retreating away. There are times when we are overwhelmed by His presence and are certain of His love. In these days or seasons, we rest comfortably in our faith, confident in our relationship with Him. At other times, we feel as though He has fully retreated from us like the ocean at low tide. We might have the sense that we are standing alone on a dry shore.

Our feelings do not determine or change God's nature. Just as the waves of the ocean never cease to tumble to shore, God's love will never abandon you. He never leaves you alone. This delicate dance of abiding requires that we trust His unfailing presence and move toward Him in prayer despite feeling as though He has gone missing.

Jesus pursues you even as you think you are not worthy of His love and attention. He longs, even thirsts, for your attention and affection rather than your fear filled obedience. Jesus uses so many things in your life to speak to you and is unrelenting in His desire to capture your heart. He speaks in the feeling of awe you experience in nature, the sense of being known as you read His Word. He comes to you in the Mass and Sacraments. He sends other people and events in your life to draw you closer to Him. He might even use your dog.

Jesus does all of this in an effort to capture the imagination of your heart and win your love. He seeks you out in order to fill you with all of the grace you need in order to experience His peace. Jesus is calling out to you, "Come away with me, rest in My Unfailing Love." Are you ready to say yes once again to His invitation?

Questions

1. What does a person or pet do who pursues?

2. Have you ever considered that Jesus is pursuing you?

3. What would it look like to love Jesus as wholeheartedly as our dog/ pets seem to love us?

4. We don't often think too much about Jesus being a real person with whom we could have a personal, intimate relationship. The type of relationship characterized by physical touch and knowing glances, similar to a dating relationship. What practice can you incorporate into your day that would allow you to connect with Jesus, and embrace Him in a spiritual sense?

5. Describe who Jesus is to you. Take some time with this one. Think about all of the women you have seen Jesus meet so far. How does He speak to them and treat them?

6. Does your image of Jesus align with the qualities of love we have studied so far?

7. Jesus pursues you in ways that cause your soul to respond to Him. How has Jesus been pursuing you? Does He pursue you through the feeling of awe in nature? Through the arts, music, etc.? Does He pursue you through your deep connection with other people?

8. Does it make you uncomfortable to think about being pursued by Jesus?

Gratitude

Rejoice always. Pray without ceasing. In all circumstances give thanks,
for this is the will of God for you in Christ Jesus. 1 Thessalonians 5:16-18

Name three women you know who have been a model of belief for you whether
it was their persistence, their patience, or their outspoken belief in the power
of God to answer prayer. Say a short prayer of thanksgiving for their example
and inspiration.

1.

2.

3.

Scripture

This is how all will know that You are My disciples,
if you have love for one another. John 13:35

The first woman we meet this week in Scripture reveals much about the heart of Jesus. Diving deep will help us to see that humbly remaining engaged with Jesus in conversation is vital if we are to learn to abide with Jesus.

Before Jesus' encounter with the Canaanite woman, He answered the scribes and Pharisees from Jerusalem as they protested His apparent rejection of the traditions of the Jewish faith. He leaves the conversation with the men who should have recognized His divinity and enters the area inhabited by the Gentiles, where He is welcomed by an outsider, a woman who believes in Him.

As you read this passage, imagine Jesus walking along the dusty road with his band of followers. They are clearly outsiders among the Gentiles, yet they are a large enough group to attract the attention of the people as they pass by. Jesus' reputation as a healer and teacher must have extended into this region as He is immediately recognized by a woman.

The Canaanite woman shows us that patience is needed to remain in conversation with Jesus when the answers we receive are not what we expect. She was intuitive and open, listening to what He said not only to her, but to His disciples as well. She did not believe that she was disqualified from receiving the gift of His healing by virtue of the geographical accident of her birth.

She did not give up and did not take Jesus' silence as His final answer. Her faith in Jesus exceeded the faith of the Pharisees, the ones Jesus thought He was sent to serve. She ends her conversation with Jesus by laying at His feet just as a puppy who trusts her owner would lay down to be petted. Her physical posture of adoration reveals a heart that is open and available to Jesus. Although she begins by yelling her requests to Jesus, her patience and persistence ultimately lead her to whispered adoration.

Read Matthew 15:21-28

1. What word does Matthew use to describe how the Canaanite woman approached Jesus? Does she appear desperate to you?

2. Do you think she was close to Him or far away? Why?

3. What titles does she use when speaking to Jesus?

4. Is she asking for Him to cure her or is she interceding on behalf of someone else?

5. How does Jesus respond?

6. Who speaks to Jesus next?

7. Why do they approach Him, what do they ask?

8. Who are the lost sheep of the house of Israel?

9. The woman must overhear Jesus talking to His disciples and is not willing to take "no" for an answer yet. What actions does she take?

10. After her first requests are met with silence, her request changes. What does she say in verse 25? What is her physical posture?

11. What is the food of the children in this passage?

12. Who are the dogs?

13. The woman continues to remain engaged in a conversation even after Jesus has seemingly insulted her. She transforms His insult into a deeper revelation regarding the relationship between God and His people. When compared to a dog, she agrees with Jesus and goes one step further saying that she wants to be the favorite pet that is given treats under the table during the meal. How does this conversation reveal her faith in Jesus?

14. How does Jesus respond to her profession of faith?

15. Falling short in the progress in our spiritual life that we hope to experience can often be related to our lack of patience, persistence, or perseverance in our prayer life. Where do you think you struggle the most today?

Read Luke 18:1-8

16. Why did Jesus tell this parable?

17. The widow had no-one to protect her interests so she needed to get help from the judge in order to obtain what was rightfully hers. Did her persistence change the outcome of her case? Which verse reveals your answer?

18. Jesus tells us that God sees to it that His justice is done on earth. Luke 18:8. Is God's justice always neatly aligned with our desires and timing? Explain.

19. Does Jesus make a connection between persistent prayer and faith? What is that connection?

20. The widow was looking for justice and protection from the judge. Who is the source of your protection? Look at your schedule and identify the activities that support your answer.

Putting It Into Practice

If you have 5 minutes, Pray:

O my God! I offer Thee all my actions of this day for the intentions and for
the glory of the Sacred Heart of Jesus. I desire to sanctify every beat of my
heart, my every thought, my simplest works, by uniting them to Its infinite
merits: and I wish to make reparation for my sins by casting them into the
furnace of Its Merciful Love. O my God! I ask thee for myself and for those
whom I hold dear, the grace to fulfill perfectly Thy Holy Will, to accept for
love of Thee the joys and sorrows of this passing life, so that we may
one day be united together in Heaven for all Eternity. Amen.

St. Therese of Lisieux

If you have 10 minutes, Ponder:

In his book *Fire of Mercy Heart of the Word Vol. II*, Erasmo Leiva-Merikakis beautifully addresses Jesus' encounter with the Canaanite woman looking at each verse of Scripture. He ends with these words:

"We may say that it excellently portrays the fallen soul's search for love and healing in God. However, such a search, leading to eventual encounter and union, cannot at times be other than a grueling process of purification, since in her fallen condition the soul is by no means prepared to withstand the vehement demands of God's glory and holiness. The initial rigor exhibited by Jesus precisely intends to make the woman fully aware of the depth of her misery when left to herself. His silence and rebuff test the quality and intensity of her love and fan her desire for him. Her running, shouting, insisting, and humbly adoring are all indispensable exercises that make her heart grow in its capacity for eternal love and joy. Above all, the process is a trial of her *fidelity*, that is of her resolute unwillingness to turn to anyone but Jesus for salvation, healing, and glorification, regardless of how high the odds seemed to be stacked against her."[1]

---

1   Erasmo Leiva-Merikakis. "Fire of Mercy Heart of the Word Volume II." Ignatius Press, San Franciso. 2003. Page 448.

If you have 15 minutes, Act:

Read this quote from retreat leader Jan Johnson:

> *Silence cultivates vulnerability toward God,*
> *because silence is an outward form of inward surrender.*

Set aside a few minutes to allow Jesus to speak to you in the silence of nature. Rest in His embrace as the breeze gently touches your arms. Allow Him to tell you how wonderful He thinks you are, not because of anything you have done, but because of who you are: a valiant delight created in love. Surrender to His love.

Prayer Intentions

Eight

Power of Persistent Prayer

Behold, God's dwelling is with the human race. He will dwell with them and they will be His people and God Himself will always be with them as their God. He will wipe every tear from their eyes, and there shall be no more death or mourning, wailing or pain, for the old order has passed away. Revelations 21:3-4

Introduction

Praying with the faith of a child is easy when you are a child confident that God will deliver what you most desire. Children often find it easy to talk to and about Jesus, as if He were a dear friend. Prayer for them is as natural as a conversation with the person seated next to them. Over time, we discover that some prayers are met with silence making it more difficult to accept the unfailing love of God and believe that God can do all things.

Instead of continuing to pray, we busy ourselves handling our concerns on our own and leave prayer behind as something to fill in the cracks rather than lay the foundation of each day. If we are to become women who reveal God's love to a hurting world, we must come to truly believe that remaining faithful in prayer is a key element of abiding with Jesus.

When I was in middle school, I persistently and honestly prayed for one intention. Every night for what felt like years in a row, I begged God to hear my petition and grant the one thing that I knew would make my life better. This plea was so deeply felt that it was attached to the end of my memorized bedtime prayer that began, "Now I lay me...". I tucked my personal petition in sweetly after my list of people I wanted God to bless.

My fervent and heartfelt request was met with crickets. Silence. Nada, nothing, no answer.

This did not stop me from pursuing my quest. I continued to pray until I eventually outgrew my secret crush on this one boy and stopped adding his name to the tail end of my nightly prayer.

Sometimes time and space give us perspective on God's plans. As I walked to class almost ten years after my last secret prayer, I realized that God had different plans for my life than the script I would write. I still remember the moment that this realization flashed in my mind. I know where I was standing, can feel the heat rising from the pavement, and the sun bearing down on me. You see, that sweet boy that I had pined over all those years ago had grown up, failed out of college, and became a parking lot attendant.

In the instant that I recognized this boy, I realized that God had saved me from myself. In His wisdom, He withheld what I thought would bring me happiness. God's silence was not a rejection of my heartfelt need for affirmation; it was protection from a path that would have been filled with temptation and pain. The way God answered my prayer was not the way I expected.

I am sure you too can make a list of similar prayers that you are grateful remained unanswered in the exact way you had originally hoped. There are things in life that are shiny and catch our attention. Things that we are certain, in that moment, will fulfill us and make our life just a little bit easier. When they don't materialize after lengthy prayer, it is easy to become discouraged and walk away from our requests. In the process many relegate prayer to the category of youthful activities and abandon the practice altogether.

Sadly, as we abandon prayer, we walk away from the One that we are petitioning as well.

Do you have prayers that you have offered for years on end that remain unanswered? Prayers for circumstances that weigh on your heart, that are not being resolved in the way that you would like? Prayers that you know are aligned with God's vision. Prayers for loved ones to return to the Church, an end to violence, racism, and abortion. As the years wear on, you are tempted to think that you just got the formula wrong or you missed some secret insight about the nuts and bolts of prayer.

It might be that you did not abandon prayer as you graduated from high school, but continued to offer prayers on the nights before big tests, as you travelled to a new Cathedral, or before a doctor's appointment. Your prayer life grew and developed over the years, but, you struggle with consistency and are unable to string together a nine day novena.

It is difficult to persevere in prayer when God does not seem willing or able to respond to our requests. When our petitions are met with silence, we doubt whether God is paying attention, and we slowly drift away from these chats, which makes resting with Him more difficult. You are in very good company if you struggle with doubt and an inconsistent prayer life. The saints doubted. Your current doubt and inconsistency are not a measure of your future relationship with Jesus.

If we are to abide with Jesus, we need to remain engaged in conversation with Him in prayer. Despite my parking lot epiphany, despite that fact that I have heard over and over again that God's plans surpass anything that I could imagine for myself, I still struggle to persevere in prayer when I get overwhelmed by life. Tired. Busy. Over-sugared and under-exercised, I often need to recalibrate my prayer life. Bad things happen. I make excuses about God knowing what is on my heart and don't give voice to my concerns. Does this happen to you as well?

Most of us fall into the "doubt trap". A time where we might feel sluggish and our prayer seems futile. We don't feel Jesus can hear us or that He is interested in what we have to say. We feel foolish for trusting God to work in a situation that seems hopeless. This may happen in a stretch of days, weeks, or years when God's love does not appear to be everlasting, powerful, or unfailing. We might be confident that God loves, just not confident that He loves us.

How do you persevere when the silence becomes deafening and you are weary from time spent on your knees? When you are in the grips of doubt, it is hard to talk to God. When both feet are firmly in the doubt trap, you get tired of waiting on God and become tempted to take matters into your own hands. Instead of giving up you need three things: a new posture, fresh words, and a little help from your friends.

A New Posture.

Loving God means continuing to pray when trust and hope are elusive. There are times in each of our lives when we lose our grip on our fragile peace and might believe God is busy with other people and unable to hear our heartfelt pleas. These are the periods where persevering in prayer feels like we are wearing high heels limping toward the finish line of an ultra marathon.

It is easy to default to the path of least resistance and throw up our hands in defeat instead of lifting our hearts to the Lord. Instead of turning our hearts away from God, we must turn and walk toward Jesus. We need to acknowledge the doubt, release the anxiety of the unknown, and imagine grasping hold of Jesus' hand. This shift in perspective will give us the clarity that we so desperately need. Changing our point of view is mandatory if we are to move through the doubt and grow in our faith.

In order to see our circumstances differently, we can alter the posture of our body. Instead of sitting or kneeling, consider talking to Jesus as you lay flat on your back looking up to the sky or face down in supplication. Talk to Him as you take a walk outside. Seeing the world from a new perspective will help your heart move toward God rather than away from Him.

Fresh Words.

When our eyes are focusing on things that are not drawing us to trust in Jesus' love, we need new words in prayer. There are days when prayer can feel stale and limp. Giving voice to our doubts is important so that we can recognize what is going on rather than turn a blind eye to our situation. When our prayers are met with silence, we can borrow the words of the saints. Often, diving deep into the Psalms helps me put words to what I am feeling and reminds me that I am not alone.

A Little Help From Our Friends.

God's healing and justice often come as a result of persistent belief in the power of God's unfailing love. In the times when God feels the furthest, the times when our belief in God is tested the most, the times when we are in the most pain— these are the times when it is vital to reach out for help. These moments, when our faith is fragile, we must turn to our sisters in Christ for encouragement and a reminder that God is always good. We need to ask others to pray for and with us when we are tempted to abandon our trust.

We can look to the lives of the saints for encouragement. St. Anna Schaeffer suffered disappointment, discouragement, and physical pain. Her prayers for personal healing were met with silence. Although she herself did not receive the physical healing she sought, she experienced a profound and deep connection with Jesus in the Eucharist despite her suffering. She did not give in to the temptation to wallow in pity because her life did not turn out as she wanted. St. Anna accepted her pain and offered it back to God as a gift. God multiplied this gift transforming her prayer into healing for thousands of other people, thus expanding the reach and power of her gift to God. Perseverance in the face of all evidence to the contrary characterized her prayer life.

If you are not in a place where you are surrounded and supported by sisters in Christ, ask Mary and Elizabeth to remind you of the truth of God's Unfailing Love. Borrow Mary's faith. Pray the Magnificat over and over again until the words become your own.

Sometimes, God's answers arrive when we least expect it, other times they arrive when we are not present to witness the miracles. Regardless, the prayers we offer in our moments of greatest anguish and doubt are often our most powerful prayers.

Perseverance, Patience, And Persistence.

Each of the women we have read about so far in Scripture teaches us something about what it looks like to abide with Jesus. Our Christian faith is unique in the belief that God created us in order to enter into a loving relationship with Him through His Son, Jesus. An integral part of this relationship is prayer- the conversation of heart that connects us with our Creator. While we understand that God is always pursuing us in love, the women from the bible show us that often it is up to us to reach out to Jesus. An intentional encounter with Jesus will change your life for the better, every single time. A necessary part of the encounter is showing up.

Just as God asks us to be persistent, Jesus models persistence, patience, and perseverance throughout His ministry. He goes to the margins to speak with women who were cast out and ignored. He pushes His disciples to keep going when they want Him to rest and take a break. Jesus reveals a heart that is open to all and seeking love in return. Let us embrace our doubt and allow it to bring us to a place of deeper trust in Jesus.

Questions

1. Silence affects our prayer life. How we respond to silence is often an indication of whether we can go deeper into the conversation with Jesus. Does silence scare you or do you enjoy times of silence?

2. How do you respond when your initial requests to Jesus are met with silence just as when Jesus met the Caananite woman?

3. How do you feel about the exchange between Jesus and the Canaanite woman? Does something about it frustrate you? If so, what?

4. The conversation between Jesus and the Canaanite woman reveals a different side of Jesus than the one we normally attribute to Him. What did you learn about Jesus from pondering this Scripture passage?

5. Do you think the Canaanite woman's humble, persistent, and patient requests changed Jesus' heart or do you think He was hoping she would keep pursing Him?

6. As we will see in our Scriptures this week, Anna remained in the temple for decades praying for God to send a Savior. What do the Canaanite woman and St. Anna reveal to you about intercessory prayer?

7. What did you learn from the Parable of the Widow about the importance of praying for your own needs?

8. Do you find it striking that Jesus places an outspoken, persistent woman as the protagonist in one of His Parables?

9. How has God patiently pursued you? Think of events where you were assured of His presence. People He placed in your path who helped you connect with your faith in a new way. Maybe it was a well-timed conversation, email, or book that found you just when you needed it.

Women of Faith

Commit your way to the Lord; trust in Him and He will act and make your righteousness shine like the dawn, your justice like the noonday. Psalm 37:5-6

Have you ever thought, even for a moment, that prayer was a waste of time? Maybe you would not have phrased it that way exactly. But, there are things that you complain about that you don't bring to God because you think they are too insignificant, not worth His time, or beyond His ability to fix. While we might not verbalize these thoughts, our inability to persevere in prayer is often rooted in these mistaken beliefs.

Looking to the lives of holy women can give hope that perseverance in prayer matters to God and that remaining in conversation with Him is one way to reveal our love to Him.

Anna Schaeffer's life did not turn out the way that she originally wanted. Had she written the story of her life, she would have left Bavaria behind to become a missionary sister, traveling to a foreign land to introduce Jesus to others who may not otherwise have experienced His love. While this was clearly a noble and worthy endeavor, what ended up happening was quite different.

Although intelligent, she left school behind at 14 when her father died, going to work to help support her family. One day, she had an accident that changed the course of her life. Trying to fix a pipe that came loose from a wall, she fell into a pot of boiling water when she was washing clothes. Despite numerous attempts by doctors to heal her legs, she became bedridden for 24 years.

Before her accident, she was a prayerful girl. This did not change after her accident; her devotion to Jesus only increased. She did not allow her suffering or her confinement to discourage her. Nor did she abandon her faith in God. In fact, her accident deepened her devotion to the Sacred Heart of Jesus as she spent her days in prayer, writing spiritually encouraging letters, and sewing. As Pope Benedict said on her beatification, "her sick-bed became her cloister cell and her suffering a missionary service". Despite the incredible pain she experienced, she offered her suffering for the Church and priests. She experienced visions of Christ and Mary, suffered the stigmata, and found great joy in the Eucharist.

She was diagnosed with colon cancer in her early forties. At the peak of her pain she wrote, "The most important thing for me is to pray and suffer for the Holy Church and her Pastors. Whenever I receive Holy Communion, I fervently pray to our beloved Redeemer to continue protecting his holy Church and her Pastors, to grant me the most agonizing martyrdom and to accept me as a little victim of reparation". She died at the age of 43. God transformed her suffering into healing for others, thousands of miracles have been attributed to her intercession.

Scripture

> *I will bless the Lord at all times; His praise shall be*
> *always in my mouth. Psalm 34:2*

In Luke's Gospel, we find Anna who remained in the Temple, giving her life to God in prayer. Her dedication was rewarded as she was able to see Jesus face to face. She was given unique insight and understood His identity as the Savior. None of this would have been possible if she had not remained dedicated to responding to the unfailing love of God.

God is patient. In His mercy, He reveals Himself as love to His people. Over and over again, He reached out through the Patriarchs and Prophets to deliver His message of love. Unfortunately, His people entered into a pattern of listening, getting distracted by looking for immediate gratification, rejecting God, and returning to Him again. The Bible is littered with stories of people abandoning God despite His continual call of love.

The covenant between God and the Israelites remained in tact even after the defection of the Jewish people, because God remained faithful to His promise. Many people left the day-to-day practice of their faith in order to fit in with or live amongst people of other cultures. In their distraction, they soon forgot to look and listen for God. Many got so far off track that they no longer recognized His voice.

Yet, some remained faithful.

Anna, stands in a unique place in salvation history. Although she was a member of one of the smaller and possibly "lost" tribes of Israel, she remembered God's promise to redeem and save His people. She returned to the Temple in the holy city of Jerusalem where she spent the majority of her life in "Old Testament" times dedicated to looking for God's promised redeemer.

Then she met Him.

Read Luke 2: 22-38

1. Who allowed Simeon to recognize Jesus?

2. What do you learn about Anna in verses 36 and 37?

3. Anna was old, widowed, and from a tribe that was considered among the scattered sheep of Israel. The tribe of Asher no longer figured into the power structure of the Jewish people (Jeremiah 23:1-8). Why was Anna's heritage important enough to note?

4. Anna waited in the Temple and trusted that God would fulfill His promises to gather the lost sheep of Israel together in Jerusalem. Do you think that she found purpose and value in her daily activities in the Temple? Explain.

5. What is a Prophetess? (If you don't know, Google) Does it surprise you to see this term in the New Testament?

6. What do we see Anna do in verse 38. Is she active or passive? Silent or outspoken?

7. What does an evangelizer do? Do you consider Anna an evangelizer?

8. Even people insignificant in the eyes of the world, here a widow from a lost tribe, are significant in the eyes of God. Does Anna represent the truth that salvation through Christ is for all people? Explain.

9. Why do you think Luke includes the detail that Anna worshiped God in fasting and prayer? Why did the Jewish people in Anna's time fast? When and why do we fast today?

10. Fasting provides freedom of heart. Do you see a connection between fasting and growing in patience?

11. What do you think Anna's friends and neighbors said about her when she moved into the Temple?

Read Luke 13:10-17

Again, we see Jesus encountering a woman with a deep faith who is not quite expecting a cure to all that ails her. Jesus not only heals her, but He defends her against the leaders of the synagogue.

12. How long had this woman been ill? How did Jesus heal the woman?

13. What does the woman say? Do you think she woke up that morning expecting a miracle in her own life?

14. Does the leader of the synagogue condemn Jesus or the woman?

15. What is Jesus' response to the leader of the synagogue?

Putting it into Practice

If you have 5 minutes, Pray:

Dear Jesus, thank You for waiting for me. I am tired from all of my running and striving. I know that You hear each and every one of my prayers, requests, my pleas. Remind me that You remain present in the silence and that Your silence is not an indication of Your lack of love and affection for me. I know that prayer is a conversation with the One who loves me most. Fill me with Your strength to persevere. I want my life to be a prayer of thanksgiving to You. Make me firm in my confidence in the power of my voice. Help me to persist and persevere with patience as I pursue You. Sustain me with Your Word and Living Water as I travel along my journey back to You.

If you have 10 minutes, Ponder:

How has Jesus pursued me in the past? Where have I felt His presence?

If you have 15 minutes, Act:

Adore Jesus for at least 15 minutes this week. If your parish does not have adoration or if it is impossible for you to get to Church for adoration, change your posture as you pray at home.

Prayer Intentions

_____

_____

_____

_____

_____

_____

_____

_____

_____

_____

_____

_____

_____

_____

_____

_____

_____

_____

_____

_____

Nine

Abiding with Jesus on the Hard Days

If love is easy, then you're not doing it right. Sophie Kinsella, Surprise Me

Introduction

It is very difficult to abide or rest with Jesus when we are distracted by suffering. If you are experiencing emotional or physical pain, all of your time might be consumed with putting out fires and addressing symptoms rather than reaching the root of the problem. Sometimes our pain is physical. More often it is emotional. Unfortunately, our personal pain, when borne alone prevents us from revealing God's love to other people.

There are many things in life that we are all called upon to endure: traffic, bad weather, the flu, and if you live in the South: Pollen Season. Some aspects of life are beyond our control; regardless of the precautionary measures you take, suffering is a fact of life. People hurt our feelings, loved ones get sick, children struggle in school with learning differences, we face financial uncertainty.

While there are many good things in our lives which endure or last, we each experience some things which we wish would just end. Quite often our suffering is magnified by uncertainty. At the outset of the new painful situation, we don't know just how long the struggle will last, which often makes us feel the suffering more keenly. We are tempted to lose hope that anything about our circumstances can change as the days pass with no resolution. Whether you have been struggling with your own pain or walking alongside someone else who is suffering, you know how hard it is to hold on day after day, without an assurance that an end is in sight.

Sometimes the suffering arrives as a byproduct of our interactions with the people we love, as when misunderstandings occur. Being in relationship with other people means we will experience miscommunication, which makes remaining open to love a little more painful. Loving people is perplexing. People get on our nerves, rub us the wrong way, push our buttons, whatever you want to call it- life is hard and relationships are complicated.

As much as we want our interactions to be linear and for there to be a clear cause and effect for everything, this is just not reality. Even if you are doing everything right, there is a high probability someone in your life will think you have gotten it wrong and won't be afraid to tell you. Just look at Jesus' life, He was perfect yet His life was fraught with misunderstanding. The knotty reality of relationships makes it difficult to love God and other people.

Not all of our struggles stem from miscommunication. Sometimes, we suffer not because of anything anyone has done wrong, but because someone we love is struggling.

What Relationships Are Causing You The Most Suffering?

Is it a spouse or a child that you are trying to convince to love Jesus? You do everything you can to show them just how wonderful Jesus is, you encourage them to attend Mass with you, you pray and prompt them to pray as well. Each of your efforts is met either with stony silence or teasing. The eye rolling hurts your feelings. When you leave for Mass, alone again, they may even remind you that you are just wasting your time following the outdated teachings of an out of touch Church. Each remark cuts you to your core. As you drive away, tears in your eyes, you are not quite sure that you can keep doing this any more.

Your struggle might be a child with an addiction that you do not understand. This sweet child who was adorable just after his bath as a toddler has now grown into a teenager or young adult and you wish a kiss on the cheek and hooded towel would heal his pain. You hate that this child struggles each day to face whatever has a hold over him and you are ready to wrestle that demon to the death. Unfortunately, this is not your battle to fight. The battle you have to fight is in discerning how to respond to the child you love.

Learning to speak up when his safety is in danger and holding your tongue when he is safe but you are disappointed, smiling instead of reprimanding. Hanging up the phone after more bad news, you don't know how much longer you can keep your heart open.

Maybe you have become the emotional or physical caregiver for your parents. Because your parents are facing their own challenges, they are coming to rely upon you in new ways which are difficult. It might be more doctor's appointments, new financial decisions, or multiple conversations rehashing the same details or concerns on top of your already busy life. Caring for your husband, children, and parents is complicated. You are already worn a little thin and then your mother calls wanting to know why you did not invite her to join you for dinner last night as she casually mentions the cute pictures from the restaurant you posted on Facebook. You wonder what the fallout would be if you block her number, even if for a few days.

How we respond to suffering will affect our relationships. When we are shouldering all of the burdens ourselves, we might think there are only two options when it comes to pain: Fight or flight. Ignore it and retreat inside our own bubble or suffer through it with clenched teeth, lashing out against any innocent who happens to cross our path. Speaking from personal experience, neither of these reactions helps us navigate the choppy waters with much success. Both are usually an invitation for more problems in the future.

Participating in God's love means discovering what it looks like to remain in relationship when the process is no longer intuitive or obvious. There is a third way: The way of Abiding with Jesus—resting in the practice of prayerfully remaining with Jesus in the midst of the uncertainty, the struggle, the pain.

The Scripture passages in *Abide* are intended to remind you that just as Jesus healed the women He met, He is the source of your healing as well. You may never have considered asking Jesus to heal you. You may not think Jesus is interested in the conversations you have with other people that keep you up at night. Yet, He has the power to help and to heal if you but lay the burden at His feet and reach out to touch Him.

We discover so many reasons to hope when we are focusing our attention on Jesus rather than all of the things which bother us. Sometimes, He delivers our long awaited healing resolving the problem. Other times, He delivers peace and carries you through the turbulent waters. This respite allows you to move forward in love when alone you are not quite sure you have anything left to give. Jesus will always continue to sustain you in His love if you call out to Him. He will fill you so that you can pour out His love on a hurting world.

In order to abide in Jesus, we need to make ourselves available to Him in daily prayer rather than focusing on earning the love of the people around us. When we remain in God's Word, in daily, if not hourly communication with Him, we are gently loved and reminded that the Holy Spirit remains present with us as we go about attempting to love others wholeheartedly.

Lingering with Him, you rediscover the fact that God has created you beautifully. He reminds you that He did not call you to strive in your relationships and attempt to earn everyone's approval. Rather, He calls you to come to know yourself more fully and share your true self in love.

It is with Jesus that we find the peace and solace that we are seeking. In Him we experience rest. Alone we are weak, with Him our love is uncontainable.

As we reflect on the Scriptures in our study we are reminded that:

- Jesus is the source of all healing.
- We must disregard distractions and negativity as we continue to approach Jesus in faith.
- Once healed, we need to get to work.

All Healing, Big And Small, Comes From Jesus.

The people Jesus met as He walked on this earth endured physical, emotional, and spiritual suffering. One woman suffered a hemorrhage for 12 years, the time it takes a child to complete elementary, middle, and high school. She comes to Jesus utterly depleted. As the ailing woman gets close enough to Jesus to touch Him, He turns to respond to a man who is seeking healing for his daughter. As Jesus starts to follow the man, a crowd continues to form with more people separating the woman from Jesus.

Are there parts of your life where you feel like you have been bruised and bleeding? Some painful incident that just thinking about it makes tears tumble down your cheeks. You are tired from keeping the rug placed firmly on top of this mess making sure it never leaks out to see the light of day. Like the woman with a hemorrhage, you are depleted and ready to release control to the One who can make all things new. You are ready to reach out.

Yet, you worry. What if my problems are not important enough to grab Jesus' attention? There are people whose situations are far worse than what I have been through or am facing today, why would Jesus be concerned about me? Can Jesus really touch me in a way that would ease my burden?

Our Trinitarian God continues to create, love, and redeem all things. He did not create the world and walk away. While the hemorrhaging woman touched the tassel that was hanging off the corner of His cloak, it was Jesus, not His cloak, who healed her. Despite countless unnamed people pressing in against Him from all sides, one woman reached out to Him in faith and she alone was healed. Her faith was like a magnet drawing His healing power.

Your healing might arrive at the hands of a doctor, the sacramental presence of a priest, or the compassionate ear of a friend. Instantly or over a period of years, we never know whom God will use to effectuate the next step in our transformation. Enduring the days when God feels distant, remaining open to the potential for God's grace to break through the monotony of everyday life, trusting that God is shaping our soul through our suffering will allow us an even deeper experience of His love.

Disregard The Distractions.

Jairus was surrounded by negativity on all sides of his life. At work, there were many who spoke negatively about Christ and sought to silence anyone who supported Him. At home, everyone had given up hope for a healing for his little girl and was already in mourning. Jairus risked his reputation to approach Jesus in public.

It is sometimes necessary for us to proceed forward in our faith despite the distractions and negative feedback we receive from people we love. We need to limit the things, which grab our attention and focus on what draws us back to Christ. Bring your doubts to God in prayer. Lay your distractions at the empty tomb. Place your worries in His competent hands. When our hands are empty, then God can give us the tools to do our best work.

Keep your eyes focused on Jesus. Call out to Him in prayer, reach out to touch Him in the Eucharist, pour out your heart to Him in Confession. He is right here with you waiting to pour out more love on you than you ever thought possible.

After Being Healed, You Have A Mission.

When God fashioned you in the stillness and quiet of your mother's womb, He created you to bring glory to Him by contributing in some unique way to building His Kingdom. You have a special combination of gifts, talents, and life circumstances that He needs in His fight for the hearts and souls of other people. In order to enter more fully into His work, you must allow Him to heal the parts of you, which are holding you back from loving openheartedly. Bring Him the battered and bruised parts causing you to limp along. Sit in stillness, rest from your striving and allow Him to tend to you.

Our greatest sufferings usually come as the result of miscommunications and misunderstandings. Little problems that begin like a pebble underfoot, a minor irritation, when ignored and not properly addressed can grow into a deep wound, which needs expert attention. Now is the time to embrace the healing balm of Jesus' words. Listen to Him say to you, "Arise little girl. Come walk with Me."

Questions

1. Are there people in your life who attempt to dissuade you from trusting Jesus and enduring in hope?

2. Do you struggle with trying to exert too much or too little control over circumstances in your life? How does this affect your relationships?

3. Are there any relationships in your life, which are particularly difficult; ones where you would rather walk away rather than enduring with love?

4. Often, we are confused about the true source of our healing. Who is the true source of healing? Do your actions reflect your belief?

5. What practices do you have that help you rest with Jesus?

6. When the Woman with the Hemorrhage, who we will see in our Scripture Section, approached Jesus, she had her eyes locked on Him and there was not going to be anyone who could get between her and Jesus. Where is your focus? What do you allow to get between you and your time of daily prayer?

7. Here is the truth: You have a special combination of gifts, talents, and life circumstances that He needs in His fight for the hearts and souls of other people. Do you struggle to accept this truth? How are you living out this truth?

Gratitude

Magnify the Lord with me; and let us exalt His name together. Psalm 34:4

In each of our lives, there are things we have had to bear which we often prayed would be resolved, healed, or altogether removed from our lives. While we may not recognize our gratitude for these crosses, often, what we learn from our suffering along the way eventually helps us to connect with other people. It may seem counterintuitive, but God uses our pain as a vehicle for transformation and healing not only for ourselves, but for others as well.

In giving thanks to God for our struggles, we are reminded of His power to redeem all things.

What are 3 ways you have helped other people because of your experiences enduring something difficult?

1.

2.

3.

Scripture

> *We even boast of our afflictions, knowing that affliction produces
> endurance, and endurance proven character, and proven character,
> hope, and hope does not disappoint, because the love of God has been
> poured out into our hearts through the Holy Spirit that has been given
> to us. Romans 5:3-5*

The healing of Jairus' daughter and the woman with the hemorrhage appear
in the early part of the gospels just as Jesus is beginning His ministry and
gathering His disciples. News of His healing power is beginning to spread and
crowds are gathering as He passes through town.

Read Mark 5:21-43

1. Both people seeking help from Jesus in this story are desperate. What
   is Jairus's physical posture when he approaches Jesus?

2. How does the woman approach Jesus?

3. Mark describes the bleeding woman as wanting to touch Jesus' clothing in order to be healed. Matthew 9:20, specifically says she touches the *tassel* of Jesus' cloak. The tassels on the four corners of a cloak were meant to remind the Jews of the necessity of following the Ten Commandments. (Numbers 15:39)

4. The woman possibly attributed Jesus' healing power to the holiness of His Jewish wardrobe. Once she touches the tassel, she is healed. How do we know that healing did not come from the "holy" tassel but instead came from Jesus Himself?

5. When confronted with the possibility of shrinking back into the crowd or revealing herself admitting what she had done, what does the woman do? Do you think this was embarrassing for her?

6. What does Jesus tell her?

7. There is a sense of immediacy and rushing in the crowds and the people around Jesus. Yet, He stops to take the time to speak to the woman with a hemorrhage, what does this reveal about Jesus?

8. While Jesus is healing and talking to the woman with a hemorrhage, Jairus hears that his daughter has died. What does Jesus tell Jairus?

9. It is chaos when Jesus arrives at Jairus' house, who is opposing Jesus?

10. Who goes with Jesus into the little girl's room?

11. What does Jesus say to the little girl?

12. After she gets up, Jesus gives strict and very practical orders. Why do you think that He mentions giving her something to eat?

13. How long had the woman been suffering with her bleeding? Do you think people abandoned her, worn out from all her talk of her ailments and her constant searching for a cure?

Putting It Into Practice

If you have 5 minutes, Pray:

Anima Christi Prayer

Soul of Christ, sanctify me.
Body of Christ, save me.
Blood of Christ, inebriate me.
Water from the side of Christ, wash me.
Passion of Christ, strengthen me.
O Good Jesus, hear me.
Within your wounds hide me.
Permit me not to be separated from you.
From the wicked foe, defend me.
At the hour of my death, call me
and bid me come to you
That with your saints I may praise you
For ever and ever.
Amen.

If you have 10 minutes, Ponder:

These words from St. Paul to the Ephesians.

For this reason I kneel before the Father, from whom every family in heaven and on earth is named, that he may grant you in accord with the riches of his glory to be strengthened with power through his Spirit in the inner self, and that Christ may dwell in your hearts through faith; that you, rooted and grounded in love, may have strength to comprehend with all the holy ones what is the breadth and length and height and depth, and to know the love of Christ that surpasses knowledge, so that you may be filled with all the fullness of God. Ephesians 3:14-19

If you have 15 minutes, Act:

Make yourself available to God by opening the way for silence.

When you are driving alone this week, drive in silence.

Prayer Intentions

_____

_____

_____

_____

_____

_____

_____

_____

_____

_____

_____

_____

_____

_____

_____

_____

_____

_____

_____

_____

_____

_____

Ten

Dwell in Love

For this momentary light affliction is producing for us an eternal weight of glory beyond all comparison. 2 Corinthians 4:17

Introduction

Recently, we went to dinner with our next-door neighbors and their children. For months they have been talking about sharing their favorite Italian restaurant with us, and we finally found a date that worked for everyone. Pulling up to the front door, they pointed out that the historic building where Villa Tronco is located was previously the home of the fire department back when they used horse drawn carriages. The restaurant is still run by the same family generations later, passed down from mother to daughter. As you are ushered to your seat, you see portraits of the women who have spent their lives feeding generations of people.

Our neighbors celebrate all of their milestone events over plates of pasta. They eagerly discussed the upcoming high school graduation of the youngest member of their clan and pointed out where they would sit for her upcoming celebratory meal. If the walls of that 19th century building could talk, I am sure they would have many things to share, both happy and sad. There is something special about a place that has been in business for more than 75 years.

I love restaurants where the recipes and decor remain the same. There is something comforting about returning, year after year, ordering the same meal knowing that it will look, smell, and taste the same each time. Of course it takes the right mixture of food, service, ambiance, and location to ensure that a restaurant succeeds long enough to gain a reputation and a following allowing it to endure.

Our dinner companions have been married for 61 years, almost as long as their favorite place has been in business. Each morning they start the day studying the Bible together. I am not certain if that is their secret ingredient as there are a million little things that go into making a marriage endure, but I think that it is probably part of the strong foundation of their relationship.

I wonder if the men who laid the bricks in 1868 for the building, which would house Villa Tronco, knew that their work would endure more than 150 years into the future. The same question could be asked of the family that started the fruit business that eventually became Villa Tronco.

Have you had the soul expanding experience of walking into an old church or cathedral? One where the ceilings soar to the heavens and you can sense the presence of the women who have worshiped there before you. Prayers hang in the rafters and angels wait ready to sing God's praises. Still standing after centuries, the buildings are a testament to the hard work that went into their construction as well as the attention of their caretakers necessary to maintain the structure. Built with sturdy materials in a slow, methodical manner, these buildings endure because their foundations were properly laid and their walls and roofs repaired. They remain as a container for the Holy Spirit and a place of refuge for all who call on Jesus for help.

We Want A Love That Endures.

Like the restaurant and cathedrals, we remain in relationships with the hope that our love will endure. Just as buildings are constructed with bricks or stones, our relationships are built with actions and words. Some of the bricks of our relationships are time, attention, and self-sacrifice. The mortar, which holds these together, is love.

What will people remember about us when we are gone? Should we dare to ask whether our love will endure in the memories of those we leave behind when we go to meet Jesus? Will they know how much we loved God and wanted to serve Him? Will they understand, deep in their bones, that they too are loved not only by us but also by a heavenly Father whose love will never fail?

If we want our love to endure, we need to abide with Jesus, the source of all enduring love.

Authentic Love Is Not Temporary.
In a world of fast fashion and fast food, our souls clamor for things that are authentic. We long for beauty and seek to hold on to places and people that are solid and consistent. Unfortunately, we are distracted by the siren song of new and fresh. We have all but given up hope that anything will last until next season, let alone another fifty years. With so many things being disposable in our world, we might be confused when we read St. Paul's words about love enduring all things and never failing. (1 Corinthians 13:7-8)

Without a personal experience of enduring love, many of us doubt that God's love endures. We raise our walls, lower our expectations, and minimize our goals. We run faster and starve our souls. We lose touch with what makes our heart sing and are worn out from looking for anything that will soothe our soul.

God's Love Endures.
Throughout Scripture, God is described in various ways.
- God is love. (1 John 5:16)
- He is never changing, never failing, and abounding in mercy. (*Cf* Exodus 34:6)
- He remains the same yesterday, today, and forever. (*Cf* Hebrews 13:8)
- He promised that He would never remove His love from us. (*Cf* Isaiah 54:10)
- God created all that is beautiful and the beauty of His creation points us back to Him. (CCC 319)

God's love is not some fly by night event, here one day and gone tomorrow like a pop-up shop or food truck. His love is everlasting and eternal. It is something we can trust. His love lasts. God's love is unfailing. God's love endures beyond the limits placed upon us as humans who are bound by the dimensions of time and space.

In order for love to grow, a special mixture of ingredients is needed: a little bit of kindness, a touch of patience and persistence, a good dose of humility, a heap of forgiveness, and time. Love is the only thing that remains of us here on earth after we are gone, living on in the memories created with the people we love. Now is the time to create as much love as we possibly can.

Have You Looked For Love In All The Wrong Places?

Some of the women we have seen in Scripture were looking for the answer to their problems in all the wrong places. The woman with a hemorrhage was looking for health so she spent all of her money on what would restore her to community life. Yet, all she found were con men, who sold her inauthentic remedies which failed. The woman caught in adultery looked for love from men who manipulated her into a painful trap.

Things that endure satisfy our soul's need for stability and authenticity. Unfortunately, we look in the wrong places for things to satisfy the stirring in our soul. In our disposable world, we spend more time pursuing flimsy substitutes rather than seeking the One who will meet our needs. As a result, we keep striving and searching for a solution. Sometimes the substitutes are people, other times it is work or something we buy.

We waste time gussying up our outsides while our insides slowly atrophy. We remain in superficial relationships that are characterized by transactions rather than pursuing lasting relationships with people who will challenge and support us as we become more fully who God created us to become. When the substitutes fail to satisfy our longing, we doubt that there is anything that will set fire to our souls.

Secretly, we think, we are at fault and missing something necessary because the dull ache in our hearts just will not go away. We might even convince ourselves that we are the ones who have failed, not the counterfeit object we were using to replace God's love. So, we stop short of abiding with Christ and accept the mediocre mundane rather than experience the fullness of life that God intended.

Please know this: The flimsy substitutes failed, you did not fail. You are not lacking. You have all that you need to be filled with God's love.

God Wants Nothing More Than To Fill You With His Enduring Love.

You are already a perfect vessel for God's love. Sit with this truth for a second, linger here. Jesus is the only One who can satisfy you. He is the source of your healing and wholeness. The ache that you feel is His way of calling you to a deeper, more intimate relationship with Him. You no longer need to be on the offensive, scouting out the landscape for any threats which might hurt you.

God's love cannot be purchased or earned. When we allow this truth to reach our hearts, we are able to rest from our striving and accept ourselves as He made us to be. This is a process, which takes time. It also requires our participation and openness.

Reach out to Jesus rather than something temporary. Abide with Him, dwell with Him in your innermost being. As you rest with Him, He fills you. He lights you up with a passion that will point you in the direction He wants for you to go. Following His lead, you can shine with His light and reveal His love to others who are in desperate need.

God offers all that you need to experience a magnificent life and a deep and enduring relationship with Him. You are never alone; you can let your guard down and meet Him in the stillness. Abide in His enduring love, walk with Him, and allow Him to show you all that He has in store for you.

Enduring love is not bought, sold, or earned. It is freely given and it is up to you receive to it. Once received, you can pour it out abundantly, trusting that He will refill you as you continue to abide with Him.

Questions

1. What is the difference between something that lasts and something that falls apart soon after you purchase it?

2. Does your soul respond to things that last or things that are temporary?

3. Are we distracted, as a community, by focusing primarily on outward appearances rather than taking care of the inner life of the soul?

4. When we think that everything is temporary and nothing lasts, does this affect our understanding of God?

5. When we fail to find anything that satisfies our soul, do we blame ourselves and think we are lacking something necessary?

6. How do women strive to satisfy the inner feeling of soul ache?

7. Does focusing on the never ending, never failing love of God help you to grow to trust Him with the most intimate parts of your story?

Women of Faith

*Go to the Heart of Jesus and draw from it, and when you need more,
go back to the Source and draw again. St. Madeline Sophie Barat*

*The work of interior transformation is necessary in order to become
a fitting instrument in God's hands, to work for God's glory.
St. Madeline Sophie Barat*

When our Woman of Faith was born in France in the late 1700s, the political and religious climates were fraught with tension. Factions within the Catholic church aligned with opposing political sides which ended up dividing and suppressing the faith.

Madeline Sophie Barat was born prematurely and was doted on by her mother and father. Her brother Louis received a good education and became a priest. Unfortunately, when Louis entered the seminary, Catholicism was outlawed in France, forcing him into hiding. He was eventually imprisoned. Upon his release Louis returned home and discovered Sophie helping support the family with her needlework. He took Sophie to Paris where he tutored her, ensuring that she learned to read and write in Latin and Greek.

When Sophie became an adult, her dreams of becoming a Carmelite were dashes as the French convents had been disbanded. As she waited for an opportunity to join an existing order, a priest approached her with an idea for another way to serve Jesus.

In 1800, she along with several friends became the founding members of the Society of the Sacred Heart. Their purpose was to help rebuild Christian life and make known the love of God through the Heart of Christ. Their work focused on the education of girls, both rich and poor. Over time, the group of women was recognized by the Vatican as a religious order.

As the founder and mother superior of the order for almost sixty years, St. Madeline Sophie Barat managed a teaching order of women who now serve around the world. She tended to find a middle path, rather than the strict rule more commonly found in her time.

At the time of her death, there were over 3,000 Sacred Heart Sisters with many schools around the world. Upon her beatification, her body was exhumed and found to be incorrupt (meaning it had not deteriorated after burial as was expected).

St. Sophie is a model for the power of enduring love. There were times when she faced leadership of her order alone. Navigating a world where men wrote the rules that she was forced to play by, St. Sophie found a way to succeed in a way that few women religious had before her. She faced resistance from within and without the church as well as from some of the members of her own order. Her enduring love for Jesus and others allowed her to remain faithful to her work.

Fun fact, the cute giraffe teethers that many toddlers carry now are named after St. Sophie.

Surely, I wait for the Lord; who bends down to hear me and hears my cry,
draws me from the pit of destruction, out of the muddy clay, sets my feet
upon rock, steadies my steps, and puts a new song in my mouth, a hymn
to our God. Psalm 40:2-4

We don't know much about the apostles and their lives outside of their work with Jesus. Yet, we do know that Simon Peter was married and had a mother-in-law. Early in His ministry, Jesus visited Peter's home and was taken to see the woman who was stricken with an unnamed illness, which caused a fever.

Her response to her personal miracle reveals what we are to do once we encounter Jesus.

Immediately after she is healed, she serves Him and everyone else who arrives unexpectedly in her home. She does not take advantage of her illness to absent herself from the kitchen. Nor does she make a huge fuss over Jesus. Nope, she just gets to work.

There is something about the encounter with His grace, which restores you and lights you on fire with a desire to help others. Allow Him to work in your life. Rest in His healing embrace. Dedicate the time to nurturing your relationship. And then set to work helping others in His love.

Read Mark 1:29-31

1. This is the second healing in the book of Mark. What strikes you about this passage? Why do you think this story is included, in this place, in Mark's Gospel? (There is no right or wrong answer here.)

2. This story is very short and appears almost slipped into the narrative description of a day in the life of Jesus. Can you imagine having just met this man on the banks of the Sea of Galilee and then inviting him into your mother-in-law's bedroom?

3. What is the woman's response to being healed?

4. When Peter, James and John arrive at Jairus' house, they are present for another miracle in yet another bedroom. What must they have been thinking?

5. Women lived in the margins and quiet places of society. Why do you think Jesus was healing all these women?

6. What must have these people seen in Jesus that caused them to invite Him into the most private spaces in their lives?

Self-Surrender Fuels Our Journey.

Jesus taught using parables nestling the complicated truths of faith in His Father into the confines of the details of ordinary life. Unfortunately, as time has passed, our connection with life in biblical times has become tenuous and has strained our understanding of the truths that Jesus was trying to convey. Nowhere is this more evident than in the parable you are about to read.

The Parable of the Ten Virgins is easily misinterpreted if we do not understand what each element of the story represents. I have always been confused about why the prepared virgins were unable to share their oil with the unprepared virgins. This seems contrary to the Golden Rule. I'm sure they had enough oil to go around just as there was enough food to go around when the loaves and fishes were passed. If we read this parable thinking the point of the story is to communicate the need to share, then the parable falls apart at the seams and we miss His point entirely because Jesus compliments the virgins who do not share.

Since it is not to be read literally, we must focus on the symbolism of the lamps and the oil in order to understand an important aspect of our individual relationships with God within the greater context of the Kingdom of God.

Brother Simeon, in his commentary on this parable, describes the empty lamps as the individuals themselves. "The oil in the lamps brought by the virgins, in turn, symbolized man's necessary self-surrender, which provides the essential 'fuel' enabling the fire of God's love to take hold on the earth and produce an abundance of light." This oil is set on fire by the divine love; it is not self-combustible.

The spiritual oil, which burns in the lamp, is the individual donation of her gifts, talents, and love to God. It is highly personal and non-transferrable. Each self-giving act of love keeps the oil liquid and allows it to burn with each touch of God.

Read Matthew 25:1-13

7. Jesus starts His parable with the words "the kingdom of heaven".
   What do you think He means? Is this far away or right here and now?

8. Why do you think the foolish virgins failed to bring flasks of oil?

9. What do the lamps symbolize?

10. What does the oil symbolize?

11. How do the lamps get lit?

12. Why can't the wise women share their figurative oil with the foolish women?

13. Is it important for us to come to know ourselves more fully in order, knowing when we need to replenish our oil, in order to make a more generous donation of ourselves to Jesus?

14. Based upon your reading of this parable, are faith and relationship with Jesus transferrable or individual?

Putting it into Practice

If you have 5 minutes, Pray:

O Jesus, my heart sings with praise of You. You are goodness and mercy and healing. Your love endures through all time and space. Help me to remember this as I go about my day. I want to love as You love, but I find it hard. I struggle to forgive those closest to me when my feelings are bruised. There are times when I focus only on what bothers me rather than delight and wonder in the other person right in front of me.

Fill me with Your enduring love. Release me from the grip of past resentments. Where I seek to criticize and control other people, blind me to what irritates me. Help me to see as You see, help me to love as You love, allow my love to endure as Your love endures in the hearts and minds of everyone I encounter each day. Amen.

If you have 10 minutes, Ponder:

It is easy to love those who live far away. It is not always easy to love those who live right next to us. It is easier to offer a dish of rice to meet the hunger of a needy person than to comfort the loneliness and anguish of someone in our own home who does not feel loved. St. Mother Teresa of Calcutta

Ponder this thought today.

If you have 15 minutes, Act:

Read Acts 16:1-5. Here we meet leaders of the early Church who endured much persecution and suffering for the love of Jesus. Journal your thoughts about our mothers and fathers in faith.

Or

Make a list of all of the things in your life you use as a substitute for lasting relationship with Jesus.

Prayer Intentions

About The Author

Katie Kibbe is a wife, mother, daughter, sister, and friend. A cradle Catholic from Houston, she practiced law before staying home with the couple's two children. In her younger days, she played a little tennis, made a million sack lunches, and ran a couple of marathons. Katie enjoys learning and meeting people from around the world. She is the author of several bible studies including *The Spirit of Mary*. She and her husband live in South Carolina where she waits for her young adult children to return with their dirty laundry. You can learn more about Katie at www.KatieKibbe.com.

Made in the USA
Monee, IL
07 February 2020